A HUNTER'S CONFESSION

# A HUNTER'S
## DAVID CARPENTER
# CONFESSION

GREYSTONE BOOKS
D&M PUBLISHERS INC.
Vancouver/Toronto/Berkeley

Greystone Books
An imprint of D&M Publishers Inc.
2323 Quebec Street, Suite 201
Vancouver BC Canada V5T 4S7
www.greystonebooks.com

*Cataloguing data available from Library and Archives Canada*
ISBN 978-1-55365-439-1 (cloth)
ISBN 978-1-55365-825-2 (pbk.)
ISBN 978-1-55365-620-3 (ebook)

Editing by Nancy Flight
Copy editing by Iva Cheung
Cover and text design by Naomi MacDougall
Cover photos (top) © Tim Pannell/CORBIS (bottom) © Warren Jacobi/First Light

Excerpt reprinted with permission of Scribner, a Division of Simon & Schuster, Inc.,
from *Green Hills of Africa* by Ernest Hemingway. Copyright 1935 by
Charles Scribner's Sons. Copyright renewed © 1963 by Mary Hemingway.

Excerpt from *The Buffalo People: Pre-contact Archaeology on the
Canadian Plains.* Copyright © 2005 by Liz Bryan. Reprinted by
permission of Heritage House Publishing Company Ltd.

Excerpt from *Measure of the Year.* Copyright © 1990 by
Roderick L. Haig-Brown. Reprinted by permission of Douglas & McIntyre.

Printed and bound in Canada by Friesens
Text printed on acid-free, 100% post-consumer paper
Distributed in the U.S. by Publishers Group West

We gratefully acknowledge the financial support of the Canada Council
for the Arts, the British Columbia Arts Council, the Province of British
Columbia through the Book Publishing Tax Credit, and the Government of
Canada through the Canada Book Fund for our publishing activities.

*To the memory of my grandfathers, Artie Parkin and H.S. Carpenter, and to the memory of my father, Paul H. Carpenter, hunters all, I dedicate this book.*

# CONTENTS

Preface  1

1  That Good Old Time  5

2  Skulking through the Bushes  34

3  The Forest Primeval  57

4  The Dawning of Ambivalence  74

5  Throwbacks  98

6  The Return of Artemis  117

7  The Last Great Hunter  136

8  Pleasure  165

9  Blood  184

10  The Wild  207

Sources  233

# PREFACE

I HAVE TWO reasons for writing this book. The first is personal. A friend of mine from Moose Jaw, Saskatchewan, a
poet named Robert Currie, has been campaigning for many
years for me to write a memoir. In this cause, he has been
more persistent than a brigade of telemarketers. Every time
I let down my guard, he would leap out from behind a bush
or a dumpster and pummel me with the same entreaty. "Carpenter, you should really write a memoir." "I'm too young,
Currie," I used to say. Or, once older, "I'm too busy, Currie."
Or, "Currie, why don't YOU write a bloody memoir?" So I'm
writing this memoir to get Currie off my back.

The second reason goes back to an incident that happened to me in 1995, which I have recounted in some
detail in an earlier book entitled *Courting Saskatchewan*.
In my account of this incident, which occurred up in
the bush, I wrote about goose-hunting rituals in Saskatchewan. Some years later, my publisher, Rob Sanders
(himself a former hunter), suggested that I write a longer book entirely about hunting—its culture, its history,
its adherents and detractors, its rise and fall as a form
of recreation and as a means of subsistence—a book in

which these subjects might be shaped, to some extent, from my own experiences of hunting. That original incident that I had up in the bush is recounted once again, but in much less detail. It seems that I could not write *A Hunter's Confession* without reflecting upon the incident that triggered it.

This book is filled from beginning to end with hunting stories, primarily from the United States and Canada. It recounts many a hunt from my own life and many stories from the lives of hunters mightier than I. I have written down the reasons I loved hunting, the reasons I defend it, and the reasons I criticize it. More than a memoir, then, *A Hunter's Confession* is a serious book about hunting in North America. I cannot help but notice a curious congruence between my experience of hunting and the trends we see among hunters all over this continent.

But it's still a memoir. If I appear to show a preference for the less than competent side of my adventures and spend little time on my prowess as a nimrod, it's largely because I've known the real thing: hunters who know what they're doing in the field and whose intimacy with the habitat and the animals themselves has turned into a great abiding love for and fascination with these creatures.

If you're still with me, but skeptical, you might be wondering, *If these guys love the animals as they claim, why do they kill them?* I might not answer this question to your satisfaction, but I promise that, as the story unfolds, I will never wander too far from it. I would like to come out of this process with a good answer for

myself. Therefore I have enlisted a great variety of writers, hunters, writer/hunters, and thinkers from the past
century to give me some perspective on the rise and
fall of hunting in my life and theirs. Hunting, like box-
ing, has attracted more than its share of eminent hacks,
Nobel Laureates, and Pulitzer Prize winners.

Doug Elsasser, Peter Nash, Scott Smith, Terry Myles,
Richard Ford, Ian Pitfield, Al Purkess, Raymond Carver,
Lennie Hollander, Bill Robertson, Ken Bindle, Bonace
Korchinsky, Mosey Walcott, Bill Watson, Bob Calder—
these are some of the hunters I have known. Any one
of them could have testified to my conduct in the field.
Most of them would say that Carpenter was better with
a shotgun than with a rifle; that he was a better dog than
a marksman; that he started losing it in his late forties;
that his sense of direction depended on whether he was
carrying a compass, and even then it wasn't that great;
that he was loath to try a long shot and timid around
bulls; that as walkers go, he was not bad for distance.

Readers can be grateful, then, that this is not so
much about me as about the hunt. If I accomplish only
one thing in this account, I hope it will be to narrow
the gap between those who did and those who didn't,
between those who speak well of hunters and those who
disapprove of them. You might say that I have one boot
in the hunter's camp and a Birkenstock in the camp of
the nonbeliever.

For the idea and for your patience, Rob, I thank you. I
hope you will agree that late is better than never.

And Currie, I am happy to say that your campaign
has borne fruit. By the way, I think it would be a great

idea if you were to write a book-length verse epistle on accounting practices in ancient Carthage. Better get started. Time waits for no man.

I am indebted to many people whose reflections on hunting have broadened my own knowledge considerably. Most of these have been mentioned in the text and in the list of sources at the end of the book. But I should add the names of those who helped to steer me into good habitat in order to write this book: Warren Cariou, Tim Lilburn, and Bob Calder, who are all either nonhunters or ex-hunters. I would like to thank Trevor Herriot for reading my manuscript and offering suggestions and criticism during a very busy time in his own life. I owe a debt of thanks to Honor Kever, my first reader and soul-sustainer. I must thank my editor, Nancy Flight, who rode this project through three very different drafts and whose words guided me into my strengths as a writer and away from my weaknesses. I would also like to thank the Saskatchewan Writers/Artists Colony Committee of the Saskatchewan Writers' Guild for the chance to work on this manuscript during the winters of 2007, 2008, and 2009. Our hosts were Abbot Peter Novekosky and Father Demetrius and the hospitable monks of St. Peter's Abbey, nonhunters every one. I owe a big thank-you to Kathy Sinclair, whose advice, erudition, criticism, and forbearance kept the fire going, and to my eagle-eyed copy editor, Iva Cheung. And a final thank-you to Doug Elsasser for his woodsy wisdom and for his patience with me as perpetual apprentice in the finer points of hunting.

# 1 THAT GOOD OLD TIME

*The keeper did a-hunting go,*
*And under his cloak he carried a bow*
*All for to shoot a merry little doe*
*Among the leaves so green, O.*
ENGLISH FOLK SONG

BACK IN the late 1950s, when I was in high school, I went hunting one afternoon with two friends. I had my father's shotgun, and perhaps my friends brought along their fathers' shotguns as well. The three of us had grown up playing in ravines and coulees that fed into the North Saskatchewan River valley. These ravines had always harbored a number of pheasants, but this particular ravine was a few miles safely outside of the city.

I was very keen on this day, perhaps because we three would be hunting unsupervised for the first time in our lives. It must have been a cold October, because fresh snow had fallen and remained unmelted on the ground. Suddenly the days had become shorter, and I felt ambushed, as I always did, by the failing light in the afternoons. We drove just outside the city in my dad's Chevy and got out and hiked to the edge of the ravine. We walked at the upper edge of the ravine in single file.

If my memory serves me correctly, we were all wearing rubber boots. I was wearing a hand-me-down hunting coat made of brown canvas and a bright red liner made of wool, but soft like flannel. The coat had many tears in it, some of them mended with thick black thread, lots of pocket space for shells and duck calls, and a big pouch for carrying birds. The pouch always had feathers in it, and the pockets always contained stubble and grit.

The ravine was to our left. It was lined with spruce trees up top, where we were walking, and it was stuffed with tangles of rosebush, aspen, dogwood, and willows down below. If a grouse or a pheasant flew down into those thickets, we would never find it. I am guessing that this was the first time we had ever hunted together. Bill Watson was ahead of me and Davis Elliot behind. Not long into the walk, I noticed a set of tracks in the snow, a three-toed bird with big feet, meandering past the spruce trees. My heart must have lurched at this discovery.

Frantic whispering and waving of arms and pointing. We began to peer down into the ravine as we went along. We probably realized that these tracks in the new snow had to be fresh. I was ready in that way that hunters must be when the signs are good. If you've ever watched a hunting dog approach a point, you have a pretty good idea of what I looked like.

It must have felt strange to us to hunt for pheasants in a ravine that we had explored as young boys. Back then, we had sported cowboy hats made of brightly colored straw, hankies tied around our necks, cap pistols unholstered to deal death. We had seen pheasants plenty of times, and the odd grouse, but we had more important business in the ravines. We had each other to shoot at. The pheasants of our boyhood were beautiful, startling, and irrelevant. And now they were our quarry.

My eagerness to hunt and kill these birds seems callous to me today—a little like shooting a family pet. The pheasants in this ravine were not pets, of course. They weren't our friends, but they had been our familiars, and they had lent to our explorations in this ravine a savor of the exotic. In the absence of tigers, polar bears, or mastodons, at least we had pheasants. Why do away with them?

If ever I had had this thought in the late 1950s, I would have swept it away without a moment's doubt.

"Hey, Carp, wait up!"

Davis Elliot was always saying this to me. He never seemed to be in a hurry, and I must have wondered if Davis wasn't a bit too prudent to be a kid. He was the much beloved elder son in a family of five kids. Like Bill and me, he was no good at contact sports. Davis was destined to become a golfer. His father was a doctor, and he and his younger brother both became doctors, and his three sisters were all bursting with brains and good looks and high spirits. The Elliots were the first family I ever got to know outside my own house. Mrs. Elliot was a great beauty and one of Mum's best friends.

"Wait up, you guys. Slow down! Jeez!"

"Jeez" was a word we were not encouraged to use at home. "Jeepers" would have been all right, but it was a girl's word. "Jeez" was almost like cursing, and almost cursing was almost like being a man.

Bill Watson would have slowed down before I did. He was more considerate than I or any of my friends were, a true nonconformist well before the word was known to us. I suspect that he was the only idealist of any age in our entire neighborhood. If one of us was out of line, he would say so and reason fiercely with us as to the rightness or wrongness of our actions. He preferred reasoning to fighting, which made him stand out as a moral paragon. At times he seemed to be channeling the enlightened nonviolence of Gandhi, and where that came from I will never know.

When we were teenagers, most of our radio stations, most of the movies we watched, most of the magazines in our drugstore racks seemed to conspire to turn us all into ersatz Americans. But Watson seemed magically immune to these influences. He introduced me to *The Goon Show* and *Beyond the Fringe* and a host of witty English movies. From Bill, I learned to appreciate the music of The Weavers, an American folksinging group, but they were okay because they had been blacklisted all over America for their leftist views. Bill's affable mother, Jessie, taught me the virtues of dry toast served cold with butter and marmalade in the mornings.

Now, in our teens, almost at the end of our time together in the same town, we were hunting for pheasants on the edge of a ravine we had navigated on scouting trips and family picnics. "Blasting away" is what we called it, without any apparent regret. After all, this was what our fathers did.

Bill Watson was okay about shooting a pheasant or two, but more than once he had to lecture me on the virtues of nonviolence when it came to sparrows or crows or anything nonedible. Once, in order to sight in my shotgun, I shot a sparrow, and he gave me hell for it. Since that day, I've never shot a nonedible bird. He pricked my youthful conscience as no one else could.

On the afternoon of our hunt, Watson went down into the ravine to see if there were more tracks in among the thickets, and Elliot fell behind me once again to toss a stick or two into the thickest brush to get something to fly up. I continued along the fringe of the steep ravine. Soon enough, I spied more tracks from our mystery bird. My God but those tracks were big—dinosaur tracks in miniature.

Hunters know that on some days you are the nimrod who acts as the dog and the other guys get to do the shooting and feel like alpha males. Some days, you can do nothing right. You just cannot get on track. You can't relax enough to shoot straight. You go one way, but the quarry goes another way, and you end up thwarted. But on that day, half a century ago, through no apparent virtue of my own, I was given the chance to go for glory. Elliot was well behind me, still tossing debris into the bushes below. Watson had just reemerged from the ravine, but he was looking back in the direction of Elliot, and I was now ahead of him.

The sound of wings exploded right beside me. I wheeled to the left, and there it was, a brilliant big peacock of a bird, three feet long, hurtling downhill and hauling its great undulant tail. The rooster was beelining it for the ravine not fifteen feet away, wing beats whirring with a mighty, rattling noise. I swung my shotgun up to my shoulder until all I could see along the barrel was bird, and I fired twice. Brown feathers, black feathers, gray and rufous feathers flew in all directions, and the big bird was down. I leapt after it, sliding into the ravine on my rump, oblivious to ice, pain, or danger. A minute later I had emerged from the ravine holding the great bird by the neck and grinning at my friends. In a generous twist of fate, it was their turn to envy me.

The rooster was a big one with a long barred tail that moved in flight like a flying snake. Its body feathers had an iridescent bronze sheen mottled with black and gray. Its head was bluebottle green, a glossy green that transformed into purple in the sun. It had a white ring around its upper neck and bright, fleshy red patches over the eyes and ears.

I had managed to do what hunters were supposed to do. I had swung my gun enough to follow the trajectory of the bird, and I had placed my quarry on the bead at the end of the barrel. I squeezed the trigger and felled the pheasant before it could get to the thickets below. But most of all, I had been ready and looking. Looking at the underbrush, looking at all the places I didn't want my bird to fly to, looking at the tracks in the snow, looking to see where my friends were walking.

It was my dad who showed me how to do all these things. He showed me how to carry a loaded gun safely, how to swing it in concert with the bird's flight, where to look for birds. It was his old castoff hunting coat I always wore, his gun I trained on, his initiative that took me out to Egg Lake to shoot at clay pigeons from my thirteenth year on. And it was his friends who showed me how entirely sociable a hunting trip could be.

GORDIE WYNN, HAROLD Williams, Gerry Wilmot, Bruce Massie, Richie Goosen, Fred Jenner, Ollie Rostrup, Rusty McClean. My dad was at his best when he hunted with these men. Gordie Wynn was the acknowledged leader and the best shot. Williams was the most persistent, the last man to put away his gun, and the official bartender. With his majestic moustache, and his rump planted on a shooting stick, he reminded me of an English gentleman. Wilmot was a practical joker who warmed up any room he entered. He could rattle windows with his laughter.

Dad, Gordie Wynn, and any two of the others would take an hour's easy drive out from Edmonton, go east of Camrose or southeast of Mundare, spot a big flight of mallards, get permission from the appropriate farmer, and dig their pits with garden spades. The idea was to find the biggest concentration of birdlime out on the stubble and locate right there. The last act was to lay down the decoys at night and then head for the nearest hotel for drinks, supper, and a few hours of sleep. Regardless of how much revelry they had indulged in the night before, they would rise early and try to be in their pits by about 6 AM. Four men was the ideal number. Gordie Wynn would assign one man to each direction, and they would wait for the first wave of birds to circle their decoys.

They always came home with ducks in the trunk, perhaps a couple of grouse or partridge, and sometimes even some Canada geese. In our subservient youth, my older brother, Peter, and I would be inveigled into plucking these birds, and the more we plucked, the more we yearned to do what the men had done. We were probably quite whiny on the subject.

When I was about nine years old, my dad bought my brother and me a BB gun, a classic Daisy air rifle. You poured a plastic vial full of copper pellets down the loading tube until your gun felt heavy, and then you sealed it off and levered a BB into the chamber. When you fired the gun, it made a noise that was halfway between a puff and a bark, and it gave a satisfying little kick.

Dad took us out into the country for target practice and showed us all about gun safety. Never take a loaded gun into the car. Never point the gun at a person. ("Yes, Peter, that includes your brother.") Always assume that the gun is loaded. No horseplay. Never peek into the barrel of a gun.

One morning at the lake I spotted a squirrel darting among the shrubs in front of our cottage. Could I drop that critter with our BB gun? Surely not. But . . . it was worth a try. I aimed for the head, squeezed the trigger, and the squirrel went down. Horrified, I dropped the gun and rushed to see what I had done. It lay at my feet, its body convulsing. I ran inside and sought out my mother and blubbered a confession. I expected a stern rebuke—I probably *wanted* a stern rebuke—but she was surprisingly easy on me. She had grown up in a hunting household, and perhaps these little atrocities were common enough to her, a thing that boys and men did because they were stupid.

She told me to promise never to shoot another squirrel and to go and bury the poor creature. I fetched the spade, but when I returned to the scene of my crime the squirrel was gone. Had a hawk swooped down and carried it away? Had it recovered from its convulsions and crawled off to die? Crawled off to live again?

In another narrative, our young hero might find the injured squirrel and nurse it back to health. Or like a tiny version of the Ancient Mariner, he would preach to the neighborhood children on the evils of shooting innocent creatures. But that was not the story of my life.

In the 1950s, in my neighborhood, fathers took their sons hunting. Bought them guns. Got their kids to do all the plucking and eviscerating of the unlucky wildfowl. Told them hunting stories. If a son was ever to bond with his father, this was probably the best way. It was through this hunters' fellowship that I got to know my dad, and that is how he got to know his dad. Blasting away at unsuspecting wildlife was almost the only ritual a father and son performed together. And we loved it.

If you find the term *blasting away* offensive, join the crowd.

When at last my brother and I were old enough, my dad relented and took us out hunting. This would happen once every fall, usually in early October, around the time of Canadian Thanksgiving. American Thanksgiving is inseparable in my memory from NFL and college football. Canadian Thanksgiving is scattered with memories of the World Series and hunting with our dad on the side roads west of Edmonton.

He must have made some sort of bargain with himself

and my mother that these trips were not about bringing home the birds. They were all about a father's duty to his boys—to instruct them, to tolerate their lapses without losing his temper, to spend time with them. Once we were on the road, he seemed to relax and ease up on both of us.

His shotgun was a twelve-gauge pump that he had acquired in Melville, Saskatchewan, in the late 1930s— something to do with a poker debt. As the decades rolled by, the blueing on Dad's gun faded until, by the time he was hunting with us, his gun had taken on a dull silver finish. It was a big, heavy weapon with a recoil pad, because it kicked like hell, and you had to pump mightily with your forward arm to get the next shell into the breech.

Our strategy on these hunts was to drive the side roads searching for flights of ducks and checking out the ditches and fields for grouse and partridge. The weather was often cold and sodden, or even snowy, so Dad's Chevy was not only our transportation but our refuge from the elements. My brother probably bagged a few birds during these years, but I doubt that I ever shot anything.

Our car had a radio. It was World Series time. We would be driving very slowly down a gravel road, squinting into the clover and the windbreaks on either side of the road; Dad would be lighting up or warning us against the excesses of tobacco or both; the score would be tied at two runs in the second. Dad might spot a partridge trotting into the stooks. He would slam on the brakes, and we would ease out of the car, ram some shells into our guns, creep into the ditch, blast away at least enough to send up a covey of partridge, return to the warmth of the car, and Duke Snider would have doubled. Dodgers up four to two.

There came to be a new presence in our car, our good friend Mel Allen, the announcer for the New York Yankees. He had a resonant, gregarious voice that was buoyed by enthusiasm and baseball wisdom. He was such good company that even his commercials were engaging. Every inning or so, he cued the ads for Gillette Blue Blades. The soldierly advice in these ads was entirely admirable, even for those of us who did not yet shave: "Look sharp, feel sharp, be sharp." This plan for success was somehow inseparable from climbing the corporate ladder, sparking the gals, and looking like Mickey Mantle. And the razor had evolved through the years from a straight blade and a strop to a safety razor with its own marching band. By the time I was ready to shoot my first grouse, Gillette's male chorus was proclaiming to all the world, "It's adjustable and, man, it's new. BRAND NEW!"

I hope I'm not the only one who remembers those jingles.

In 1951, Canadian culture didn't stand a chance. In the years that followed, I cheered for the Dodgers, the Milwaukee Braves, the Giants—anyone who might have a hope of beating the Yankees. When we were listening to the ball games, we were also warming up from our last foray into the blasting winds. And then Dad or Pete would spot a pond with a few mallards feeding, asses raised to the sky, mooning us and our puny guns and our presumptuous dreams of conquest, and we'd be out there sending our pellets into the void. I don't think we ever got entirely warmed up or ever heard an entire game.

Though hard to come by, the grouse and the ducks were great sport. The lunches Mum packed were great. The ball games were great. Inside or outside the car, it didn't matter: life was one continuous adventure.

IN THE FALL of 1954, Dad and his hunting buddies chipped in fifty bucks apiece, bought a small hunting cabin, and plopped it onto the shores of Egg Lake, about twenty miles north of Edmonton. They had rented the land from a farmer. Their cabin was a one-room shack with a wood stove and four double bunks. The only light at night came from gas lamps, and we had to bring our water from town. There was a biffy out back. It was a great pleasure on Sunday mornings to see Gerry Wilmot sitting on the can with the biffy door open, reading his newspaper. He was my father's perfect opposite— outgoing when my father turned shy, loud when my father was restrained, irreverent when my father was in his straitlaced mode. Mr. Wilmot had brilliant silver hair, a great abundance of laughter, and a smoker's cough that functioned as our alarm clock each morning.

One of Mr. Wilmot's contributions to the lodge's decor was a big poster of a young woman stepping naked from her shower. She was innocent looking, blonde, dripping wet, with a residue of soap bubbles on her neck and shoulders, and for reasons mysterious to me, she wore a clueless, happy smile. Why would some-one all alone and naked in the bathroom be smiling? I can't remember what the ad was for. Cigarettes? Tractor parts? But she was a beacon for adolescent yearning. It was difficult, beholding the gaze (okay, the breasts) of this smiling girl, to believe that sex could be evil. I mean, there was no question in my mind that sex really was evil, but my beliefs, in the presence of this fine example of contemporary realism, were severely tested.

When I ogled her on the far wall of the shack, I was dimly aware that we were in male terrain, that this glorious vision had no place in our house. But out here, where men carried guns, pissed in the bushes, and sought the predator within, where Mr. Wilmot was a defining presence, an outlaw world beckoned. The hunting at Egg Lake was so-so, but the experience of being there with my friends and our dogs and our dads was entirely to my liking.

I was a virgin in any way the metaphor could be deployed. I had never even shot a duck. I had potted clay pigeons Mr. Williams launched with his hand launcher, and I dreamed of the day when I would join the older boys who had already been, as it were, blooded.

My initiation into the fellowship of hunters came around the age of fourteen on a father-son hunting trip. My older brother would have been our designated young hunter, but for some reason I was chosen to come along instead. It was the first time I had ever been turned loose on anything that had feathers with anything more lethal than a BB gun. I was given my older brother's gun, a single-shot Cooey sixteen-gauge, and a pocketful of shells. I wore Dad's old hunting jacket, the brown canvas coat with the red wool lining, and a worn hat of the same canvas material.

Early in the morning a brigade of fathers and sons drove in two vehicles to a slough somewhere northeast of Edmonton. The land was owned by a farmer who was one of my dad's customers, so we had his permission to shoot over his slough. Once we boys had been stationed along the shore, hidden in the cattails, our dads drove the cars away from the area and walked back to join us.

By the luck of the draw, I must have been placed in a flyway. Most of the ducks would have to take off into the wind and wheel over by me to reach the best feed or pass my way to return to the water. No sooner had my dad returned from parking the car than I bagged my very first duck. I think it was a gadwall, a small brownish duck that looked like an undersized mallard hen. Mr. Williams's dog, a sturdy old springer named Mort, recovered my bird, and my father was jubilant.

There was a fair bit of bird traffic between our slough and some others nearby, and the men dropped a few more. And then came a moment of glory that eclipses the killing of my first duck. Some blue-winged teal came whistling right down the slough in front of me, flying fast with the wind, and I swung my gun ahead of them and fired. Two teal dropped. Old Mort hit the water running. The men went wild. I could imagine them wondering who this new prodigy was, this Deadeye Dick.

My friends would have none of it, of course, and they razzed me without mercy. For a while I was known as Two-Teal Carpy.

But when old Mort brought in those two birds and dropped them at his master's boots, I was thrilled to the roots of my being. I had found something I could do as well as the other guys, and on a slough northeast of Edmonton, my life seemed to change. I was still the dreamer who toddled along in the shadow of his smarter, more athletic older brother, but by the end of that day, I had dispatched five ducks.

Slough ducks, my dad called them. We sliced out their breasts, and Mum marinated them in the fridge for a day or two and roasted them in the oven. I was in such a frenzy of accomplishment that it was some time before I realized that Dad and his hunting pals looked upon teal and gadwall with some disdain.

For my seventeenth birthday, my dad gave me a sixteen-gauge shotgun, a cut above the Cooey single-shot. This was a Remington Wingmaster, a pump gun that was light enough for shooting partridge without blowing them to bits and heavy enough for shooting Canada geese at reasonably close range. When a flock went over, you fired and pumped, fired and pumped, fired and pumped out the last expended shell. For a few seconds the air smelled of burnt gunpowder. The mucky rotten aroma of marshes, the sharp moldy scent of stubble fields, the cordite smell of burnt gunpowder. Hunting with Dad was always an olfactory delight.

My Wingmaster was the greatest gun I ever owned. My friends had heavier guns, twelve-gauges and occasionally ten-gauge shotguns. Some of them owned more prestigious weapons—Browning semiautomatics, for example. Some of them hunted with European double-barreled shotguns with engraved steel and beautifully carved stocks and butts. Often they bagged more birds than I did, but I clung with gormless pride to my

Wingmaster. I brought it out almost every fall for thirty-six years.

THE DAY CAME when Dad and Mum decided they could finally afford to buy a cottage. The shack at Egg Lake passed into other hands, and in 1958, my parents bought a small lot at Ascot Beach on Lake Wabamun. The following year, Dad purchased the old dental clinic from a defunct air base at Edmonton's Municipal Airport. It was just an empty wood-frame building about the size of a large garage. It cost Dad five hundred dollars for the building and a thousand dollars to have it moved out to Ascot Beach, forty miles west of Edmonton.

By this time I had finished high school. Our hunting trips took off from Ascot Beach to somewhere in the parkland north of the Yellowhead Highway. We always teamed up with Dad's friend Mr. Massey and his son, Bruce Jr., who, like me, was starting out at university. The families would gather at the cottage on Thanksgiving weekends. My mother and Mrs. Massey would spend the day gabbing and cooking the big meal, and the males of both households would head north of the Yellowhead for a day's hunt. Sometimes we came upon ruffed grouse in the ditches filling their crops with clover, or sharptails in the fields pecking at the swaths of wheat and barley. Sometimes we encountered a covey of partridge; they were such fast fliers that they were nearly impossible to hit. One of Dad's clients had a pheasant farm somewhere northwest of the lake, and the farm went under. All the remaining stock was released into the countryside, and we had a go at those as well. For the most part, the hunting was pretty good.

One fall, however, we drove the side roads and walked the hedgerows and couldn't find a bird worth shooting. This is often the fate of the weekend hunter. If he doesn't live where he hunts, he is frequently unaware of the cycles of growth and depletion that determine what is available for hunting. He walks for miles in his favorite beats, and if he sees any game birds at all, they are flushing out of range.

"Well," said Mr. Massey on that day, "it's just nice to get outdoors and do some walking and breathe that good air." We all nodded in agreement without the slightest conviction.

"How'd it go, hunters?" my mother said when we returned.

Long faces, shrugs, grunts.

"Well, nobody asked me how *my* day went," said she.

There was a familiar smell coming from the kitchen—I mean, in addition to the aroma of roasting turkey. A wild fragrance that we should have recognized. She had our attention.

"Well, I'm glad you asked. Muriel and I were having a cup of tea, sitting right at this table, when we heard a big thump on the front window."

She shot a thumb in the direction of the thump.

"What was it?"

She went over to a small black roaster on the stove, lifted the lid.

"I don't believe it," said my dad.

"My lord," said Mr. Massey.

They were staring at a nicely done ruffed grouse.

"Seriously now," said my mother, with her flair for cheekiness, "how did the hunting go?"

THE IDYLL OF father-son hunting was not to last. A father wants to hunt with his sons forever, but how long can a son remain fixed in that supporting role? We wanted to drive the car and call the shots and prove to ourselves and to our father that we were much more than just his boys.

For me the split came in the fall of 1961, when we three Carpenters and a couple of friends were hunting sharptails and mallards out by the Glory Hills. After a great deal of walking, we all returned to the car for a drink and a snack. I was the last to return. By then there were six or seven boys and men hunkered down by the vehicles. I leaned my shotgun against our car's bumper. My safety was on, but I still had two live shells in the chamber. I was gulping down some water when my father came up to check on my gun.

"Is that thing still loaded?" he said.

I caught an edge to his voice.

"Yes."

"You've got a loaded gun leaning against the car?"

"The safety's on," I said.

"What the hell do you think you're doing?" he said. My father would never use the word "hell" in his boys' range of hearing unless the situation was pretty serious.

"What if a bird flew over our heads?" I said. "Like this morning." Surely my logic was unassailable.

Apparently not. With my brother and the other hunters looking on, my father lit into me with all the fury and sarcasm at his command.

"Of all the lame-brained, stupid stunts to pull," he began, and his tirade continued until his lungs could hold out no longer. I can't remember the words, but I can still hear the iambic rhythm of his many tirades. Of ALL the LAME-brained STU-pid...

Clearly he had no second thoughts about humiliating his son in front of his friends and mine, and he expected me to take it, as I always did. He must have known, at least dimly, that we were all afraid of his temper. The thing that galled me most, however, was that he was probably right. I had done a careless thing with the very gun he had bought me for my birthday. I had let him down.

His ferocity, his sarcasm, my ignominy were all too much. For maybe the first time in my life, I yelled back at him, and he flinched. I don't remember what I said. It would be tempting for me to cast this confrontation as my bad-tempered father against his sensitive young son. The most disquieting fact to me, however, is the way in which my counter-tirade must have replicated his own. It is never particularly comforting to discover that some of the flaws that bothered me about my parents have resurfaced in me.

THE LAST TIME I hunted with Dad was about a decade later, in October of 1971. There might have been a trace of atonement in it, at least for me. By then he'd had a bad heart attack and carried his nitro wherever he went. His angina was especially touchy in the cold weather, and he puffed and wheezed when he walked any distance.

Hunting around Edmonton had changed for Dad and his friends. They could no longer pop over to Camrose or down to Mundare for a quick shoot. They had to head almost all the way to the Saskatchewan border. This was around the time that Alberta premier Peter Lougheed was sending out press releases and giving speeches alluding to the province's embarrassment of riches. Oil rigs dotted the countryside, and Alberta was in one of its periodic booms. Edmonton and its satellites had expanded into the countryside with merciless speed. The great flights of mallards that I had seen as a boy were a rarity, at least where I lived and hunted. But one Sunday evening when Ian Pitfield, Terry Myles, and I were coming back from a hunting trip up north, we noticed a huge flock of mallards pitching into a large weedy slough, which was surrounded by barley swath. There was no evidence of hunters around, so we asked the farmer whether we could return to hunt on his land. He was only too happy to see someone drive off the birds, so I took down his number and promised to get back to him.

It turned out that my hunting pals were busy, but this location looked ready-made for my dad and me. There was good cover down by the slough, and that meant no pits to dig. But where would we bunk the night before the shoot? There wasn't a hotel within twenty-five miles.

"Are you sure about the location?" my dad said.

"I'm positive," I said.

"And you've got permission."

"Of course," I piped up. "I've just talked with the farmer on the phone, and he says the slough is ours. The birds are still there."

"You're sure."

"Positive."

My dad had an idea. He would ask Richie Goosen to come along and to bring his truck with the big RV in tow. Goosen's trailer had plenty of room for the three of us, and there was a bathroom with a flush toilet. We could make breakfast over a propane stove, and best of all, we could walk from the trailer to the edge of the slough in five or ten minutes.

It turned out to be a pretty good plan. When we arrived in the evening there were thousands of ducks, mostly northern mallards, fattened up on farmers' grain. Goosen parked his big RV on a rise above the slough among a grove of aspens and a thick belt of berry bushes. We were close enough to the birds to observe them without scaring them off. The weather was warm for October. It would be nippy in the morning, with a tinge of frost, but the sun would warm things up for us as the morning progressed. We decided to walk the three hundred yards or so to the edge of the big slough, fan out, and hide in the willows, cattails, and bulrushes that grew in great clumps well out from the water's edge.

Richie was a great rotund bald man with a booming voice and an unflappable regard for his own opinions. He was a millionaire several times over, a handyman and a civil engineer, and he owned both a construction company and a small drilling outfit. But he was a blowhard, and my mother loathed the sight of him. Dad had always defended Richie, and my mother did her best to go along with it. Dad had been his broker, which meant that there had been a healthy bit of symbiosis going on between them. Goosen, I imagine, was the sort of business dynamo that made the Alberta economy tick during those years. I think Dad admired him for his entrepreneurial energy and his great optimism. Whenever he landed a big contract or struck oil up in the Swan Hills or somewhere west of Red Deer, he passed cigars around. But by the 1970s, when Dad had at last retired, Richie had acquired a tendency to bully my father. This was painful to watch, because my father was in shaky physical condition and looked a lot older than I'd ever seen him before.

The sun had not yet risen when we stumbled out of Goosen's trailer. We headed toward the slough together for a minute or two, then spread out with Dad in the center so that he would have the shortest distance to walk, Goosen on the left flank, and me on the right. I walked fast because I wanted to be sure I was lying in good cover before the mallards began to move. I didn't want to be the one to scare off the first flight of birds.

The light that heralds the sun a few minutes before it rises through the mist is the color of clear tea. If you look through the bulrushes and focus your attention just above the mist and listen hard for the whistle of wings, you might just see the first flight of mallards rising out of the marsh.

A small flight appeared in front of me, skimming the calm surface of the water and heading my way. I waited till they were almost upon me, and then I rose up, swung my shotgun just ahead of the lead bird, and fired. It spun into the water a few yards to my right. Then a whole great raft of mallards quacked into the air and flew in front of us, over us, to the left and right and behind us till the air was whistling with the sound of their wings, and we fired again, all of us, one after the other, *whump, whump, whump-whump,* into the mayhem. It was quite a moment. It is always quite a moment.

I waded in and collected my first mallard and looked back to see where a second one had fallen. That's when I saw my father, standing halfway between Goosen's trailer and the marsh.

"Come on down," I cried to him. "It's better down here."

"It's okay," he called back. "I'm fine up here."

I retrieved my other duck and saw Richie retrieve one as well.

"Won't the ducks see you up there?" I cried to Dad.

"I'm just fine here," he said again.

It occurred to me that he didn't want to come any closer to the marsh because he would have too far to walk back up the hill to the trailer. His angina would not allow this small liberty. While Goosen and I were thinking about ducks, my father was thinking about mortality.

As the morning progressed, the ducks flew higher and higher, and by the time they passed over my father's head, they were out of range. He got off a few shots, but he didn't do any damage. I had a sinking feeling that my dad might never shoot another duck.

AT SUPPER THAT night in Goosen's trailer we had a rousing discussion about the hunters' quarry. The best I can do is attempt to reconstruct the last part of our conversation. I am working with the rawest of materials. My father's thin voice, his frequent need to clear his throat. Goosen's resonant bellow, his glowing pink pate. My presence in this discussion as the self-appointed naturalist and bleeding heart.

We had shot a dozen or so mallards. My father claimed that this flock was the biggest he'd seen in quite a few years.

"Not as many birds around," he said.

"Oh," said Goosen, "there's lots a birds around. You just have to drive farther to get them."

"Not so many pintails," my father said. "Canvasbacks."

"The pintails are in decline," I said, and I told them about a wildfowl census report I had read. The decline had something to do with new cultivating techniques. The pintail nests in the fields were getting plowed under each spring.

"There's lots of pintails," said Goosen. "I seen some last week over by Drayton."

"Not like it used to be," said my dad. "Ten, fifteen years ago, we'd always come back with a few pintails. There was a mating pair last spring at the cottage. Prettiest birds in flight you ever saw."

"Not bad eating, either," said Goosen.

"And look at the driving we did yesterday to find these mallards," said my father. "We never had to drive this far before."

"So we drive a little farther. Gas is cheap."

"I'd hate to think what this place will be like when we've destroyed the best marshes and wiped out all the ducks," said my father. "The fall won't be the fall anymore."

"Way you shot today, Paul," said Goosen, "there's no worry about lack a birds."

My dad tried to laugh it off, but it seemed to me that this was a low blow. After the first hour of shooting, my dad had simply given up.

"Here's to many more of these shoots," said Goosen, and now the whiskey was beginning to proclaim itself and he was yelling. "Because dammit, Paul, we'll always have ducks to shoot. Pintails, mallards, or whatever. Because no way in the world could we wipe out these critters. Too many of em. You don't believe those gov-mint reports, do you, David? I'm surprised you'd get taken in by that."

"When there were scads of prairie chicken," I said, "that's what they used to say."

"There's lots a chicken," said Goosen.

"There's sharptails," I replied, pedant to the last. "But what about the pinnated grouse?"

"The what?" said Dad and Goosen simultaneously.

"The pinnated grouse is the true prairie chicken. Used to be lots of them down on the prairie till we destroyed their habitat. Now they're extinct in Canada."

"That's just what I mean," shouted Goosen. "Gov-mint propaganda. They want us to think that so's they can shut us down anytime they feel like it."

But I would not be shouted down. Even though I was getting tight on Goosen's excellent Scotch and sleeping in his sumptuous trailer, I would not be cajoled into agreeing with him. I was drunk on my own pedantic wisdom.

"When the herds of buffalo darkened the prairie," I said, "when the great flocks of whooping cranes blackened the skies, that's just what they used to say."

"Useta say what?" snapped Goosen.

I quoted him word for word. *"No way in the world could we wipe out these critters."* I paused to see if my parody of Goosen's words had struck the target. My father winked merrily at me. "But where are the buffalo now? Where are the whooping cranes?"

"Gone with the dodo birds," said my father.

"What in the hell is a dodo bird?" said Goosen, who by this time must have realized that he was outnumbered by Carpenters.

AFTER THAT DAY my dad quit hunting, and he began to seek out the birds with his binoculars and to build birdhouses out at the lake. His journals all through the 1970s and 1980s are filled with observations of weather and birds. He became a yearly contributor to Ducks Unlimited. So have I.

Ducks Unlimited. Sounds like Richie Goosen's version of reality, doesn't it? We would not need this excellent organization if duck populations across the Great Plains were once again healthy and unthreatened. But the pintail is now disappearing from the prairies. You have to drive to southern Alberta, North Dakota, or southwestern British Columbia to see flocks in any numbers. With its chocolate-brown head, long slender neck, and long tapering tail feathers, the male pintail is the most elegant duck I've ever seen.

The mallards are with us yet. The drakes are decked out brighter than Little Richard. Yellow beak, orange feet, dark blue feathers on light brown wings, opalescent green head with a white collar and a chestnut-colored breast. They can make their nests in beaver dams, river valleys, city parks, even sewage lagoons, but their numbers are well down from that good old time in the 1950s.

The huge flocks of whooping cranes that were said to darken the prairie skies are just a rural myth. The great white cranes had a stable population in the presettlement days, but they were never that abundant. However, evidence suggests that they might be coming back from near-extinction. It depends which year they are counted.

The dodo of Mauritius was wiped out by hunters. Not even a single reliable specimen of the dodo remains. We have only a few preserved fragments of its skeleton throughout the world and a few drawings done by rank amateurs.

The image that brings me back to Richie Goosen's trailer more than thirty-five years ago is that wink my father gave me. I cherish it to this day.

I have been cherishing a lot of my past lately, rolling around in nostalgia for a good old time when *blasting away* at birds with a shotgun was considered an innocent pastime. But hunting has come under fire these days for the best and worst of reasons, and grappling with some of those reasons is one of my motives for writing this book.

Sport hunting is in decline in North America. So is subsistence hunting. Sport fishing is in decline. Outdoor activity in general is in decline. The more we talk about the environment, the less we see of it. Says Nicholas Throckmorton, a spokesman for the U.S. Fish and Wildlife Service, "What we're seeing among young people is, in a phrase, nature deficit disorder." There are some exceptions to this general trend—my own province of Saskatchewan, for example, where the numbers of hunters have increased in recent years—but I cannot quite decide whether this increase in hunting activity is a good thing.

I never asked such questions when I was a young hunter. The problem with innocence, of course, is its blindness to the moral implications of our acts. The problem with that good old time is that it is gone, and I am left to wonder just how good it was. We live on an imperiled planet in which humanity swarms all over the earth, compromising the land as it goes, the water, the air, the very climate at the distant poles like a metastasizing cancer. Whatever escapes getting tamed by us gets consumed by us.

Nevertheless, when I examine deer tracks or grouse tracks in the snow, these things still awaken in me: the slight increase in heartbeat; the riveted attention; the awareness of sounds and smells; the patient, highly focused scanning of the bush around me. I am driven to ponder where this response comes from, and that is what the next chapter is about. But before we plunge into the ancient origins of hunting, I have to say this: cherishing the act of hunting for wild animals has become more and more difficult for me. My memories of the thrill of the hunt are tempered more and more with regret. If Bill Watson were around to hear my confessions, that is what I would tell him.

## 2 SKULKING THROUGH THE BUSHES

*Meat eating helped make us what we are in a physical as*
*well as a social sense. Under the pressure of the hunt,*
*anthropologists tell us, the human brain grew in size and complexity,*
*and around the hearth where the spoils of the hunt were cooked*
*and then apportioned, human culture first flourished.*
MICHAEL POLLAN, *The Omnivore's Dilemma*

HAVE OFTEN wondered where my sense of urgency for the hunt came from. I suppose it came from my father, because he nurtured it in me. Or, genetically speaking, it came from his father, who loved to drive a buggy to the outskirts of Regina and shoot sharptails during the first quarter of the twentieth century. Or, more to the point, because we are talking about *urgency*, it came from my mother's dad, Artie Parkin, founder of the Saskatoon Straight Shooters, circa 1920 to 1940, a club for men to teach youngsters how to handle guns and hunt wild game. My dad and his Edmonton friends were keeners, but Artie Parkin was said to be obsessed.

Not only do I wonder what woodsy legacy brought my father and me from Edmonton to Richie Goosen's trailer to hunt mallards in October of 1971; I wonder what historical phenomena made it likely that fathers in Alberta would buy firearms for their sons and take them hunting. I can see this paternal legacy being passed on from generation to generation in settlements up north among the Cree and Dene hunters, but we were middle-class white folks, and Mr. Noaks, our friend the butcher, provided us with all the meat we needed to get through the winter.

My quest for answers to these questions has sent me a long way from Edmonton, Alberta. It began in Scotland, in May of 1970, with a conversation I had with a woman who was a hunter herself and a member of the English gentry. We weren't hunting, but we were both guests at a gentleman's hunting lodge in northern Scotland. She was talking to me about the grouse, deer, and pheasants that people over there hunted each fall. The conversation featured the usual differences in nomenclature. We hunted bucks, for example, which they called stags. And we hunted pheasants without using gillies or beaters.

"And we don't *hunt* pheasants—we *shoot* them," said she.

"What's the difference?"

"Well," she said, "one doesn't visualize oneself skulking through the bushes to shoot a pheasant." Clutching an imaginary shotgun, she went into what I thought was a provocative crouch. I think she might have been going for Yosemite Sam in pursuit of Daffy Duck. "I mean, you people, you seem to fancy that sort of thing."

She seemed to be calling upon centuries of cultural superiority to make her point. When she and her tribe did a-hunting go, they stood in a designated shooting area waiting for the pheasants to be released by the thousands. After the gamekeeper's big release, the beaters would keep the pheasants flying until the affair was over. The skulking through the bushes in search of pheasants was the job of the dogs and the hirelings. This distinction between hunting and shooting is an important one. You might say that this exchange between the lady and me at least suggests, if not encapsulates, the history of hunting.

When we take a look at the lady's ancestry, or indeed my own—I mean around two million years ago, at the time of the first true humans, *Homo habilis* ("handy man"), so named because these hominids had learned to use stone tools—we discover that as a species we had evolved into gatherers, scavengers, and occasional hunters. Without a hint of apology, we skulked around in the bushes looking for food. The much-debated *hunting hypothesis* of human origins came from scientific ruminations on the remains of these people. The theory goes that when one branch of apes learned to wield (throw, swing, carve) weapons to kill their prey, they were able to turn away from a diet of fruit and vegetation and become successful carnivores. Thus, they ceased to be apes and took the road to humanity. Hunting separated them from the lower orders of apes; hunting made them human. This theory of man as killer ape, however, has not gone uncontested over the last few decades. Indeed, as far as researchers have been able to discover, the animals these early humans ate were probably more scavenged than hunted down and killed.

If we examine the dietary evidence of hominids a mere million or so years ago, we discover that hunting for food has begun to complement scavenging as a source of food. Presumably, our *Homo habilis* had learned a great deal about predators during their millennia as scavengers: how to find the kill sites, when to scavenge and when not to scavenge, how to avoid the predators, and perhaps even how to defend themselves against these creatures that sometimes left their food sources unguarded. The same dietary evidence, however, indicates that plants are still the major food source for our gatherer-hunters.

By the time the skills of these hominids allowed them to take the offensive and hunt large mammals, they had evolved into bigger, stockier beings—"erectines," as the paleoanthropologists call them. (*Homo erectus* is the variant we have come to know best.) The erectines, with their ever-more sophisticated stone tools, pursued the great migrations of large animals from the African continent to the Eurasian continent approximately 700,000 years ago. Like the great predator cats, they pursued elephants, hoofed animals, hippos, and smaller mammals simply because they were an abundant food source.

One of the most evolved branches deriving from the erectines was the Neanderthals, who hunted in Europe until about 35,000 years ago. They constitute the least fortunate branch of the human family (*Homo sapiens neanderthalensis*). They were probably not blessed with the genetic makeup to survive the last great ice age to its conclusion, and they became extinct.

Another branch of *Homo sapiens* emerged as the dominant species, what we, in our vanity, like to think of as the end result of erectine evolution. This emergence began somewhat before the last great ice age, perhaps as early as 140,000 years ago. These ancestors too were gatherer-hunters and are thought to be anatomically modern human beings. They are not credited with inventing fire, but their use of fire was so widespread that it came to define them as the modern humans who survived the last great ice age. They continued to evolve and flourish through the late Paleolithic age (the classic stone age) right up to the advent of agriculture.

Their period as consummate hunters reached a peak around the end of the late Paleolithic age, which saw the rise of the Cro-Magnons. They were the big-game hunters of Europe. Much like the diet of modern caribou hunters of the Canadian North, more than half of their food was meat. These ancient cold-weather survivors, the Cro-Magnons, managed to maintain populations all over Europe and northern Asia and later in North America. The quarry was large mammals—mammoths, horses, buffalo, and caribou. And as the availability of big-game animals began to diminish, the ingenuity of the hunters appears to have increased.

I am talking about the Mesolithic age, from approximately 20,000 to 9,000 BC. This is the age during which agriculture began to develop in isolated pockets around the Middle East. But until agriculture took over as the major source of food for tribal societies all over the world, including North America, hunting became increasingly high-tech. The hunters of the Mesolithic era had learned, over the millennia, to hunt in groups and to deploy weapons such as spears and, later, bows and arrows.

Hunting historians who reach the Neolithic age must surely lapse into melancholia, because they are then forced to concede that hunting for subsistence is losing its chic. Around 10,000 BC, the populations of the tribal units on several continents had grown considerably. This population growth coincided with the end of the ice age. With more mouths to feed, tribal groups turned to growing plants and corralling hitherto wild animals. The agricultural revolution took over as mercilessly as a swarm of McDonald's franchises. Hunting and gathering could support one person per ten square miles. But the farming and animal husbandry that characterized Neolithic agriculture could support about one hundred times that many people.

With the obvious success of advanced hunting techniques, and with the disappearance of traditional habitat owing to the end of the ice age, the great mammals that had fed populations of *Homo sapiens* for so long went extinct. From dietary evidence gathered at tribal sites of the Neolithic age, we can see a dramatic shift from meat to wheat, barley, legumes, fruit, and nuts. For humans, the age of the Big Meat was relatively short, lasting from about 35,000 BC to perhaps as late as 10,000 BC. There were some big exceptions to this trend, Aboriginal hunters on the Great Plains and in northern Canada and Alaska being among them.

There is some strong evidence that this radical shift from meat to grains and fruit in the Near East, Western Europe, northern Asia, and scattered parts of Africa precipitated a widespread decline in human health. Communicable diseases sprang up, and with the drop in iron levels, anemia and osteoporosis proliferated. The height of early Neolithic peoples declined by about four inches from that of the hunting tribes of the late Paleolithic age, and poorer nutrition seems to be at the heart of this decline.

And so hunting, this time for smaller game animals, continued along the fringes of many tribal groups like a counterculture. In Israel, from the Hakkarmel burial sites, archaeologists have unearthed a stone-age culture from about 12,000 BC. These people, the Natufians, were hunter-gatherers until they collided with the agrarian and herding cultures. By the time of Moses, circa 1250 BC, the Natufian hunters had been wiped out.

As far as we can tell, this seems to have been the fate of most, though certainly not all, hunting cultures throughout the world. In the Near East, around 12,000 BC, hunters began to corral gazelles for later consumption. In Syria, between 11,000 and 10,000 BC, the diet radically shifted from wild gazelles to domesticated goats and sheep. By about 8500 BC, this shift was complete. Around 7000 BC, in what is now Mexico, deer hunting and seasonal plant gathering gave way to maize cultivation. In South America, evidence suggests that Andean tribes cultivated wild plants as early as 5000 BC. Agriculture spread widely after it took hold in this region, and hunter-gatherers began to trade wild meat for beans, maize, and potatoes. The spread of agriculture stopped in the far south, where growing seasons were short.

In large areas of the Near East, China, Thailand, Meso-America, and North Africa and parts of southern Africa, hunter-gatherers and agrarians managed to live side-by-side and trade wild game for plants. Whenever wild game and seasonal plants become scarce, however, hunter-gatherers inevitably would become dependent on agrarians. The agrarian cultures grow as their lands grow, and the hunter-gatherer tribes tend to shrink.

As grasses and grains began to flourish at the end of the last great ice age and spread throughout the world, the agrarian way of life began to dominate, resulting in the fall of hunting. The agrarian mode gained momentum when it became clear that hunting and gathering, and the nomadic life that went with it, was an arduous and doomed existence.

By about AD 1500, hunter-gatherers still retained a hold on about one-third of the world's land mass (Australia, the northwestern half of North America, the southernmost part of South America, isolated regions in central and southern Africa, and scattered parts of Asia). But the agrarian producers had expanded at a steady rate and commanded the best soil and land for growing and for horticulture, and they had access to the best water. The remaining hunters were frequently stigmatized and marginalized until at last they were seen as the enemy.

The hunter-gatherers who began colonizing North America, however, from about 12,000 to 11,000 BC, were probably more fortunate than other nomadic hunting cultures in their choice of hunting grounds. According to recent theories, they might have been preceded by a contingent of hunters who first settled on the islands of the West Coast around 15,000 years ago. But the largest, most prolific colonists are believed to have descended from Alaska along a newly opened corridor, freed from ice, as though eternal spring had at last been declared.

The first of these people arrived about 11,000 BC at the northwesternmost extension of the Great Plains and gathered, yes, around my hometown of Edmonton. Well, it wasn't quite Edmonton back then. The great hunters descending from the Bering land bridge and Alaska would search for evidence of Wayne Gretzky in vain. But in that place where, as a young man, I began to wonder where my dad and I had acquired such an avid taste for the hunt, the first pioneers gathered and multiplied, and their newfound success had much to do with hunting.

In *Guns, Germs, and Steel*, Jared Diamond tells us that, at this time, the North American West looked like "Africa's Serengeti Plains . . . with herds of elephants and horses pursued by lions and cheetahs, and joined by members of such exotic species as camels and giant ground sloths." The great wealth of Clovis sites tells us that these huge mammals were hunted with bow and arrow and with impressively large spears. Indeed, the bulkier, more exotic mammals were hunted to extinction. The Clovis hunters continued to follow their quarry southward into the Americas, and as the largest of the mammals began to disappear, various groups of hunter-gatherers evolved into agricultural communities.

This evolution of agricultural settlements was modest and very slow, because in vast areas of the Americas, such as the Great Plains, there was a lot of buffalo and not much of an incentive to move on from hunting and gathering. Hunting cultures persisted into the age of the railroad. For about ten thousand years, their main quarry was the bison. Liz Bryan, in *The Buffalo People*, put it this way:

> Seldom in the history of the Earth has a single animal species had such drastic influence on humanity. Without the bison, it is doubtful if people could have existed at all on the arid plains; certainly not in the way that they did. For the bison was much more than a food source; its hide provided shelter, clothing, shoes, bedding and blankets; its bones were made into tools for shaping stone, scraping hides, working leather and for sewing; its sinews and hair were twisted into cordage; its horns, bladder, paunch and scrotum were used as containers; its dried dung was indispensable as fuel on the treeless plains. Tied inexorably to the movements of the wild herds . . . the people became nomads, following the source of their sustenance in daily and seasonal cycles from the high plains in summer to the shelter of the foothills and valleys in winter. If the herds prospered, the people prospered; when the herds failed, the people starved.

BRYAN RECOUNTS THAT the bison occupied a central role in the mythology of the people who lived off these animals. In their creation stories, the buffalo was an object of worship as the ultimate source of life. These stories constituted a kind of oral scripture that included tales of people and bison intermarrying, which seemed to suggest a mutual ancestry of the two species and the all-encompassing symbiosis between humans and buffalo. Just as the hunting peoples of the Far North maintained a strong spiritual connection to the caribou, so the hunting peoples of the Great Plains were strongly connected to the buffalo.

It is tempting to wonder if, out of this bison-centered religion, a conservation ethic might have come into play. Like all the emerging hunting peoples of the world, the people of the northwestern plains killed as many buffalo as they needed to feed their hungry. Unlike the great ice age mammals that were hunted to extinction, however, the great herds of buffalo seemed to go on and on into eternity—as though the animals and their hunters had struck some sort of balance. At their peak, the bison were said to number fifty to sixty million animals.

On the Great Plains, for perhaps ten millennia, the people hunted buffalo on foot with spears, atlatls, and bows and arrows. They would frequently hunt in large groups on the prairie above river valleys, first alarming the great bison then driving them over the edges of steep inclines known as buffalo jumps. At the bottom of these jumps, the foot soldiers, men and women, waited to kill and butcher the crippled animals. Where there were no river valleys or steep coulees, the hunters built buffalo pounds in dips and declivities in the prairie. Above these walled-in corrals made of stone, the men and women would pile rocks on both sides of the run to guide the bison toward the pound, which the animals could not see. The hunters then drove the animals into a wild stampede, and some of them would run into the pound and be slaughtered by waiting hunters with bows and arrows. A pound could contain two or three dozen animals. The weapons were like miniature longbows, some of them less than three feet long, tillered from chokecherry trees, green ash, maple, and even the trunks of saskatoon berry bushes.

This kind of hunting was dangerous, especially driving the bison, which was done on foot. The drives suddenly became more efficient when horses were introduced from the south, about a century after Columbus made first contact. Horses did not reach the northwestern plains in any numbers, however, until around the end of the seventeenth century. By a process of tribal rivalries and trading by Aboriginal groups, the horses made their way north to the Canadian prairie.

It was primarily the Shoshones, kin to the Comanche, who brought the horses north as part of their conquest of the Great Plains. For a long time, the Shoshones, and their greatest allies the Crows, were the dominant tribe on the central and northern prairie. Their horses were first deployed in the buffalo hunt, but by the early eighteenth century, they were enlisted in battle. The Shoshones, with their mounted warriors, presented such a terrifying spectacle that they sent the Cree and Blackfoot north in droves.

The Cree and Blackfoot didn't take long to acquire horses and learn to ride them. They took even less time to trade their goods for muskets, metal tools, and other weapons with the French and English traders. In a decade or so, the Shoshones were sent packing, and the buffalo hunt, the high-tech version of it, spread over the northwestern plains.

By about 1730, the hunters on the Great Plains were able to use horses to herd buffalo to the edge of the jumps instead of doing all of this work on foot. They had learned as well to work with the dogs they had domesticated to help with the hauling. Now they could chase the buffalo and shoot them with muskets or, if not exclusively with muskets, with steel arrow and lance points. The bow-and-arrow hunters still had a big advantage over the musket hunters, because a man with a musket had only one chance to kill a buffalo. By the time he had reloaded, the entire herd would have stampeded away from him. Arrows were silent and accurate, and a good hunter could loose many arrows in a short period of time.

The buffalo were at last driven from the land on the Canadian prairie around 1890. Again, it is difficult to find any evidence of efforts to conserve the bison herds. Native hunters on the grasslands discovered that they could trade for guns, steel arrow points, and tobacco with pemmican. This dried-meat-and-berry mixture was in high demand by the voyageurs, who found it very nourishing. It was usually made from buffalo meat. Eventually the bison hunters were able to trade for repeating rifles, rather than the single-shot muskets of the early eighteenth century. Thus, a party of hunters with breech-loading repeating rifles could kill more bison by shooting them from a greater distance than a party of bow-and-arrow hunters could hope to kill.

Here is a case in which prehistory collided with recorded history in the tragic transformation of a great Aboriginal culture. The moment that hunting buffalo turned from subsistence to commerce, Native hunters began to slaughter bison at a hitherto unheard-of rate and did so more easily because of improved weaponry.

The great Métis hunters of the late eighteenth and the nineteenth centuries were probably even more efficient in their slaughter of the bison than their grasslands Aboriginal trading partners. They entered the pemmican and buffalo hide business in a big way, and they were able to carry away their hides and meat on Red River carts and sell them en masse to the fur traders. These big-wheeled carts could convey considerably more buffalo hides than any travois.

The incoming settlers from Red River, Manitoba, to Fort McLeod, Alberta, were just as culpable in the destruction of the ten-thousand-year-old buffalo hunt. They wanted farmland and ranchland, not roaming herds of buffalo. And if the buffalo sustained the nomadic bands of Aboriginals across the northern prairie, then a good buffalo was a dead buffalo. Indeed, defeating the Indians by exterminating the buffalo was U.S. domestic policy. Sport hunters on both sides of the Medicine Line blasted away at bison from flat cars, leaving their victims to rot in the sun.

And last, but certainly not least, were the traders from the south. Primarily white buffalo hunters traded in buffalo hides to supply the leather industry and to meet the demand for buffalo robes throughout the

United States. They slaughtered buffalo, abandoned the meat, and floated their hides with great efficiency on flat boats and small barges down the Mississippi River. The hides were used, among other things, to make belts to run factories in the East, and one of the uses for the bones was to manufacture bone china.

If prehistoric bison hunting with bow and arrow was skillful, organized, and life-sustaining, commercial bison hunting and agriculture were devastating. Nomadic Indians could not coexist with European agriculture. Without the political will from white settlers and sportsmen to save the bison, the animals were driven to near-extinction. The last of the great herds died with the meat still on their ribs, and the stink from their unharvested carcasses was unforgettable.

Wildlife conservation? Such a civilized and curiously modern expression. The dream of bleeding-heart liberals and animal lovers like me. But it was out of the question then. As we shall see, the first great strides toward wildlife conservation came from unexpected sources.

Some remaining fringes of hunter-gathering tribes found their last chance in the Far North, among the great caribou hunters from Alaska and the Yukon to Labrador and northern Quebec, where white civilization was less intrusive. Small pockets of Aboriginal hunters can still be found within a few hours' drive from where I write these lines in northern Saskatchewan. But the horses are gone and the sled dog teams are fading fast, and the children of our last great hunters are pursuing their animals throughout the long winters on snowmobiles.

HUNTING FOR FUN is a relatively recent idea in our history as a species. First, we had to have leisure societies, buttressed by agriculture and trading, wherein the powerful few learned to celebrate hunting as a game. The earliest evidence of sport hunting comes from Thebes, in Egypt, during the mid-fourteenth century BC. Perhaps for the first time in recorded history, kings and noblemen hunted bulls, lions, and other large animals from chariots drawn by small horses. They brought along their retinues, bowmen and barmen with beating staves, who wounded and exhausted the prey so that the man in the chariot could finish it off.

I suppose the lady I spoke with at the hunting lodge in Scotland several decades ago might be tempted to imagine her ancestors on the chariot while mine were wielding a bow and arrow in advance of the chariot or beating the bush to put up something noble, like a lion or a stag. But in her eyes, on that evening in 1970, I was something of an anomaly. In her England, the men who skulked through the bushes like Yosemite Sam were called poachers. I don't want to give the impression that I was therefore more closely aligned to the great hunters of the Mesolithic era than she. After all, in my native Canada, I was never hunting primarily to feed my family; I hunted for the adventure of it.

This is the kind of hunting we tend to read about. In my forays into the hunting section of the public library here in Saskatoon, I have discovered three rows of books (about ten feet of solid pages). There are books on target shooting with rifles, shooting varmints, shooting deer (many of these), and on shotgunning for quail, ducks, grouse, doves, geese, and clay pigeons. There are books on archery and black-powder rifles. There are anthologies (sometimes referred to as bibles) of hunting stories, by which I mean bang em 'n bag em stories, of great hunts throughout North America, and travel books on safaris to Africa and other continents in search of trophy heads.

But in this library, one of the most intensively used in all of North America, on any given day, there are a mere dozen or so books on those same shelves that have nothing at all to do with the how-to approach to sport hunting, nothing at all to do with the glory of the conquest, one well-heeled nimrod to another, bragger's rights to the biggest trophy head and all that hairy-chested stuff. These dozen volumes rest on the shelf like lepers at a bus stop. David Petersen's *A Hunter's Heart* is one such book. The stories he has anthologized here all demonstrate a strong empathy for the wild creatures the hunters pursue. Invariably, the writers are conservation-minded people (Jimmy Carter, Tom McGuane, Edward Abbey, Jim Harrison, Ted Kerasote) who happen to love hunting. Rick Bass's *Caribou Rising* is about defending an Arctic caribou herd, the Gwich'in hunting culture, and the wildlife refuge that is their home. James Swan's *In Defense of Hunting* is a Jungian analysis of the sport hunter's psyche.

These brave dozen or so are misfits among the shelves of hunting books in the 799.2 section. They are, let's face it, nerds among jocks. At night when all the patrons have gone home, I can well imagine that the great army of how-to books and safari adventure books gang up on the sensitive ones and call them names that impugn their masculinity.

My point is that the sheer bulk of hairy-chested-gentleman hunting literature generates the illusion that sport hunting is in some mysterious way superior to subsistence hunting. I am tempted to believe that the writers and readers of this material consider that subsistence hunting, done mostly by Aboriginal people throughout the world, is not only less interesting and less heroic but less appropriate in defining the hunting narrative of our time.

Indeed, the paleoanthropologists of the next few centuries may well turn their attention away from dogsled and snowshoe cultures in the Far North and descend upon the dismantled and buried suburban malls and their sporting goods emporia, seeking out evidence of the great hunters of the early second millennium, the primitives who stirred fossil fuels into the mix. The people who hunted from cars along the side roads as I did with my father (*Homo automobilis*). The more sophisticated men who transported all-terrain vehicles in trucks and set them loose on timber roads because of their loathing for walking in the woods and fields (*Homo out-of-shapiens*). And of course the northerly tribe of hunters who were so evolved that they could run down deer and coyotes to exhaustion in the deep snow and shoot them (*Homo snowmobilis*).

SPORT HUNTING IN North America aspired to be the sport of kings. The Theban chariots may well have evolved into jeeps and all-terrain vehicles, but sport hunting in North America evolved from one kind of feudal system or another. In various European countries, members of the landed gentry could secure hunting rights on vast estates, but their tenants had to poach their game to feed themselves. In North America, hunting for sport came out of the earliest leisure societies on plantations, ranches, and wilderness forests. Not only was it one of the privileges accorded to the landed gentry, but it came with the conquest of the land, the westward march of American and Canadian settlers, and the rigors of pioneer life. Hunting in North America developed into a beloved pastime that combined the gentlemanly appeal of golf with the shoot-em-up savor of the Wild West.

By the late seventeenth century, trappers, traders, and commercial hunters had spread out all over the North American continent in search of beaver, buffalo, bear, moose, and anything else of commercial value. As these incursions increased in the eighteenth and nineteenth centuries, the impact on wildlife became catastrophic. As we have seen, the buffalo declined to near-extinction. The plains grizzlies all but disappeared. The last remnants of this population sought refuge in the Swan Hills of northern Alberta, and their future there is in grave danger. The passenger pigeons completely disappeared.

If there was one man who came to define hunting for sport in North America, it was Theodore Roosevelt, renowned trophy hunter, scientist, historian, war hero, naturalist, and politician. He embodied the whole tradition, from hunting to fill the larder, as early settlers had done, to hunting on safari for trophies. From his experiences of hunting, especially in the American West, he became the popular embodiment of the great white hunter. When he finished his years in the White House, he went on safari to Africa, where he hunted from Kenya to the southern Sudan. There he managed to kill at least two of every species of animal that he could find. At least two is putting it mildly. For some species he went as high as eighteen trophies. His total bag was five hundred and twelve. Let me put that in numbers: 512 dead animals. He must have seen them all as Democrats.

But Roosevelt was also one of North America's most influential conservationists. He worked hard to establish strict laws to protect wildlife from being slaughtered by hunters who had no love for the animals they pursued. He fought, with real success, to protect wildlife habitat by helping to establish national forest reserves, national parks, and zoos. The following credo, written by Roosevelt around 1910, was thought to be a rather progressive stance at the time:

> I never sought to make large bags, for a hunter should not be a game butcher. It is always lawful to kill dangerous or noxious animals, like the bear, cougar, and wolf; but other game should only be shot when there is need of the meat, or for the sake of an unusually fine trophy. Killing a reasonable number of bulls, bucks, or rams does no harm whatever to the species; to slay half the males of any kind of game would not stop the natural increase, and they yield the best sport, and are the legitimate objects of the chase. Cows, does, and ewes, on the contrary, should only be killed (unless barren) in case of necessity.

POACHERS WERE ROOSEVELT'S enemies. Sportsmen from influential American families were his friends. He hunted with the social elites of the Boone and Crockett Club, which he helped found, but he also hunted with wranglers and squatters. He combined the traditions of the European aristocrat and the North American maverick. His hunting ethic and his example were very much alive in my father's memory, an orthodoxy to which many sport hunters belonged. In a profound and pervasive sense, the boys and men of America in the first half of the twentieth century and beyond were all skulking through the bushes with Teddy Roosevelt.

This brief history of hunting leaves us with two traditions: subsistence hunting and hunting for the fun of it. Both traditions survive to this day and face off along the shrinking habitats with a persistent level of antipathy. But between the two traditions are vital connections that should not be ignored. Some Native people, for example, have turned to sport hunting in recent years, and non-Aboriginal people engage in subsistence hunting as well.

Aldo Leopold, the naturalist from Wisconsin, who hunted for subsistence and for the fun of it, considers both sport hunting and subsistence hunting in his classic *A Sand County Almanac* (1949). He reminds us that Aboriginal culture often coalesces around the pursuit of wild game. Among (largely white) people who hunt and fish for the sport of it, the cultural landscape is very different, but the culture manages through hunting to reengage with its wild origins by renewing contact with wild things. From hunting, Leopold tells us, hunters can affirm three important cultural values.

First, "there is value in any experience that reminds us of our distinctive national origins and evolution." Leopold sees this awareness as "nationalism in its best sense." He doesn't talk about nationalism in its worst sense, the history of wholesale slaughter and conquest that seems to be part of the colonial heritage and does not need to be reenacted. Instead, he gives us examples that may well have come from his own boyhood: a boy scout has "tanned a coonskin cap, and goes Daniel-Booneing in the willow thicket below the tracks. He is re-enacting American history." A young boy who traps rodents is "re-enacting the romance of the fur trade."

The second cultural value derived from hunting and other engagements with the wild is "any experience that reminds us of our dependency on the soil-plant-animal-man food chain, and of the fundamental organization of the biota [Leopold's term for living organisms in the environment]." Leopold quotes a nursery song about bringing home a rabbit skin "to wrap the baby bunting in." This folk song is Leopold's reminder of the time when human tribes hunted to feed and clothe their families.

Leopold concludes with a third cultural value: "any experience that exercises those ethical restraints collectively called 'sportsmanship.' " These restraints might have been learned in the company of more experienced hunters, but they are enacted in solitude. The hunter "ordinarily has no gallery to applaud or disapprove of his conduct. Whatever his acts, they are dictated by his own conscience, rather than a mob of onlookers. It is difficult to exaggerate the importance of this fact."

As a young hunter exploring the wilderness twenty years after Leopold's death, looking back on my own experiences of hunting in the United States and Canada, I can see obvious reasons why the split between the two hunting communities has been perpetuated. But I can also see a great deal of truth in Leopold's conclusions about the two traditions. Having read him so recently, perhaps I am a bit closer now to explaining the depths of excitement I shared with my dad, my brother, and all our hunting buddies who gathered in Edmonton more than ten thousand years after the arrival of the first hunters in North America.

## 3 THE FOREST PRIMEVAL

*I like the gun. It is a familiar thing, full of associations. I am a different man when I am carrying it, more alert, more careful, more purposeful than without it. Carrying a gun has taught me a thousand things about animals and country and wind and weather that I should not otherwise have bothered to learn, has taken me to a thousand places I should not otherwise have seen . . . Killing has a place in hunting, if only a small one. I see it as a rite, a sacrifice, an acknowledgment of the sport's origin that gives meaning to what has gone before. But never as an end in itself.*

RODERICK HAIG-BROWN, *Measure of the Year*

IN THE mid-1960s, when I began skulking around in the bushes with my hunting buddies, I did not see my activities as springing out of an evolutionary process or a culture of hearty hunters, or, for that matter, any other culture. My only awareness of Teddy Roosevelt had to do with his bushy moustache and his alleged use of the word *bully,* as in, "The boys and I had a bully good hunt." I was bent on pleasure and on paying off my student loans and not much else. Bringing back the details of that life is not easy for me. But one hunting trip seems to have burnt its way into my memory.

It started with a party at someone's apartment in the fall of 1967. A friend of mine suggested that we go on a wilderness river trip during the October long weekend. I was probably not sober, and probably everyone in this jammed apartment was my best friend, life was a simple proposition, and so, why not? In my quest to discover all the things in life that were deemed to be far-out and to avoid all the things in life that were not, the response to this suggestion seemed an easy yes.

By the time I had regained sobriety, however, the thing was set and I could not back out. My friend, Scott Smith, had planned it out to the last detail. He and I were going to run the Wild Hay River, camp along the way, and hunt big game. We would butcher our quarry and carry it out in two boats.

"Why two boats?" I asked him.

"You ever loaded a bull elk onto a single canoe with all your supplies and everything?" he said.

I had never butchered anything bigger than a jackrabbit, and I had never heard of the Wild Hay River. It flows clear and icy out of Rock Lake, which is just northeast of Jasper National Park, through heavily forested hills and muskeg in the shadow of the eastern Rockies. The first half of its descent from the lake is rapid; the second half, where it crosses Highway 40 to join Moberly Creek, is meandering. We would be doing the first half.

Yeah, whatever. Why not?

We drove three hours west of Edmonton, then up along the Grande Cache road toward the source of the river, just southeast of Rock Lake. We dropped our boats and equipment under a bridge, drove back down in both vehicles to an abandoned ranger station where the river crossed a gravel road, and left one car there. Then we drove together back up to our boats.

I had never camped in wilderness, never hunted for big game, never owned a rifle before, almost never tented in freezing weather. By the time Scott and I approached the bridge where our gear was stowed, the afternoon sky had darkened and the wind had risen. We parked the car by the little bridge and locked it up. Scott went about packing his canoe, and I loaded up my two-man rubber dinghy. I can remember no conversation. Perhaps the steady roar of the little river would have drowned it out. Everything we did in that cold fifteen minutes or so was done with a strange finality. Every little chore (securing my sleeping bag and my clothing inside a couple of garbage bags, placing my oars in their brass-lined holes, checking to see that my rifle was unloaded) seemed to move me to the brink of the irrevocable. I remember looking at a stretch of white water that tumbled between two boulders and seeing, for the first time that day, snowflakes pelting the shoreline.

*Oh, Jesus.*

There is a moment on a river when you seat yourself in your boat, push off, and begin to row or paddle, and you feel the irresistible pull of the current. The bridge, your car, the road—they all seem to drift away from you, and you are overcome by the disconcerting and delicious realization that finally *you have no choice.* This was the first time I had ever felt that sudden release from all comfort and all fear. There was simply no time for fear. My buddy up there in the canoe cannot help me. There is that white water to the left as our boats careen down the river at the mercy of gravity and that rock on the right and these oars in my hands. As I faced the river for the first time, I saw quite suddenly that these oars were meant to defend me from getting swamped. The banks of the river flew by, and I realized that—*hey, these oars work!*

A word about my oars. In Edmonton, the cheapest camping and fishing equipment was found at the Army & Navy Department Store. Sometimes the deals you got there were too good to be true, and my inflatable dinghy and my oars found their way into that category. These oars were about four feet long and made of aluminum. Whenever I took the boat out fishing, the palms and fingers of my hands would turn gray.

Less than a mile downriver from our launching bridge, I followed Scott over a churning great tumble of white water and flew backward into some rocks by the shore. I cannot remember exactly what happened, but I came away from the collision with one oar in my right hand and the blade of the other oar in my left hand. I don't recall what happened to the shaft or how I managed to grab onto the blade. But there I was, waving the blade and hollering to Scott to put ashore in his canoe.

We both managed to scramble up the bank and drag our boats to safety. In the midst of too many difficulties to recount (snow, wet clothes, cold wind, unfriendly river, you name it) there was this broken-off hunk of blade in my hand with an empty socket where the shaft had been, and somehow this had to be made back into an oar.

Scott remembered an abandoned wooden shed, perhaps from a logging crew. In the driving snow, we headed for the shed to catch our breath and retool. I suppose we could have dragged all of our gear back up through the forest and found the road and our car and gone home. But something foolish and wonderful must have happened in that first tussle with the river—something that made both of us not merely determined to carry on but high on adrenaline.

I dug around inside the shed and found some old shingle nails. Two of them were straight. I pulled a large jackknife out of my pack, another cheap affair from the Army & Navy but new and therefore reasonably sharp. I ventured out of the shed and found a recently fallen young aspen that must have been two or three inches through the middle. I carved away at the tree at both ends until I had a staff about four feet long. I had to slice off the bark and peel away some shavings, but at last my piece of aspen fit into the socket at the end of the blade. With a flat-edged rock I pounded home the two shingle nails. They went through the cheap aluminum as though it were tinfoil.

In the meantime, Scott must have been back out in the snowstorm rearranging our loads. I showed him the repaired oar, and we both laughed at it. We might have been a half hour from hypothermia, but in our present situation we thought my new oar was funny. That's what it was like to be a twenty-five-year-old city guy who grew up reading Zane Grey, Roderick Haig-Brown, and *Outdoor Life*. There was no quit in us, even when perhaps there should have been.

I had stripped down to my shorts and T-shirt because my outer clothes were sopping wet. Back into the river we went, and the snow came down in big wobbly flakes. The last thing I noticed as we were pulled into the current was our shabby old shed. It was the last sign of civilization we would see for a long time.

We couldn't see the mountains for the falling snow. We could barely see fifty feet ahead. But my funny oar worked just fine. And so, in our separate boats, we hacked our way down the river a mile or two until the light began to fade. By the time we found an open and level place to pitch our tent, the darkness was coming on with alarming speed. I was shivering in my shorts and T-shirt, grappling with my two garbage bags filled with clothes and sleeping bag. I was desperate to get into something dry and warm. I dumped the contents of both bags onto the ground, picked through them, and discovered very quickly that everything, even my sleeping bag, was sodden.

Scott did not have this problem. His canoe had remained relatively dry. Perhaps he'd also had the good sense to double-bag his supplies.

Hypothermia, yes. This was a word that had not yet entered my vocabulary, and thank God for that. One less thing to worry about. But what was I to do? I began to drape my clothes and my sleeping bag and its canvas cover over the branches of trees. I was vocally shivering, like a man with a bad stutter, and wincing every time a bare foot came down on a sharp rock.

But suddenly there was fire. That's my next memory. A big hot fragrant crackling campfire. Where did that come from? How did Scott build a fire out of wet wood? Had he broken off some dead branches from a sheltered tree when I wasn't looking? Had he cheated and brought a small can of gasoline? Was this friend of mine some kind of woodsy prodigy? I simply don't remember.

What I next remember is that we put up the tent, a big canvas one, and it was dry on the inside. And we ate something from Scott's cooler. And we were standing by the fire drying out our clothes. It seemed pretty late at night, and the snow had stopped, but the wind was still blowing and the temperature plunging.

I was wrapped up in my ancient sleeping bag and turning like a roasting wiener in a bun. The sleeping bag, an old Arctic-gauge goose-down bag enclosed in a canvas wrapper, was a gift from my uncle Stan. My uncle had used it in the Far North when he was training to go overseas to fight in the Second World War. No zippers on the bag, just metal snaps. The closer I brought it to the fire, the more it got singed and gave off a smelly vapor and took in smoke. It began to smell like the aftermath of a house fire.

Our conversation must have been a little eccentric. How does one wiener address another when the first one is constantly revolving around a spit? Does he wait for that moment when he is facing his friend? My guess is that Scott did most of the talking. He was so keen to hunt the next day that the prospect of freezing to death seemed a mere inconvenience. He was probably at that point reminding me of the limitations of our tags, which we had bought with our big-game licenses. We would shoot an animal and immediately secure the tag around a tendon in its back leg.

"Why immediately?"

"Game wardens."

"So, when we've done all that, how do we haul our moose back to the boats?"

"Elk."

"Oh, right. What if we shoot an elk or two and we have to haul the meat through all this bear country?"

Scott was silent for a moment. He grinned at me as I rotated back into sight.

"Just pray we don't shoot anything till about the third or fourth night out."

We must have fallen asleep in a tent full of smoky clothes, many of them almost dry. I was all wrapped up in a sleeping bag singed by the fire. But it was warm and comfortable, and I was as dry as a burnt hot dog.

THE MORNING WAS chilly, and the snow lay everywhere on the ground, inches thick. It weighed down the pine and tamarack boughs. But the sun rose bright, and by the time we'd had our breakfast, the day began to warm. Scott went off with his rifle to check the ground for elk sign. I fetched my cartridges from my packsack and my rifle from its case and checked it out for signs of moisture.

I didn't like the guns my friends used to bring down deer, elk, and moose, because these guns had scopes, and to my eyes, they had little heroic appeal. For this trip, driven by ignorance of the hunt and by a streak of romanticism, I had purchased an old saddle gun, a 30/30. It had a dull, brown walnut butt and stock. It held six cartridges in the breech and one in the chamber.

You pulled back the hammer for the first shot, fired, and pumped the lever with a quick forward thrust of your trigger hand. This is a bush gun, ideal for shooting in heavy forest because of its short barrel and peep sights. You don't have to locate your target with a scope; you just line up the sights with the animal and squeeze the trigger.

The Daisy air rifle that my dad had bought my brother and me was built in the likeness of this 30/30 saddle gun. It's a small weapon, but if you know how to shoot, you can stop a large animal at two hundred yards. In my case, eighty yards was more like it. But while my friends were squinting through a scope, I was communing with all the cowboys in Hollywood.

I loaded the gun and began to swing it up to my shoulder, picking out targets in the bushes across the river. One such target had dead branches that had dried to silver over the seasons. The branches spread out with a nice symmetry, almost like antlers. An easy shot. I was about to swing at another tree when this one seemed to dip its head. I looked again. My dead tree was a bull moose. It must have been gawking at me for some time. I had an elk tag, and there was no way I could have convinced a game warden that I had just picked up the wrong tag or mistaken a moose for an elk. There were no game wardens for fifty miles in any direction, but somehow this didn't matter. I raised my gun and imagined bringing down this great animal. He was up on an incline across the river, looking down at me. He stood hemmed in by thick spruce, and the dark brown of his body made him almost invisible in the deep shadows. But his antlers could not be disguised, and they stood out from the moose like the upturned palms of a giant.

"What are you aiming at?"

Scott had come up behind me from his morning excursion.

"Something I can't shoot."

Scott put the scope on the big bull. He was impressed.

"We've got elk tags, right?"

"Right."

"Not moose tags."

"Right."

"So we can't . . ."

"Right."

We broke camp after lunch and loaded up the boats. We had a lot of river to run in the next few days, and Scott had found no signs of elk at our first camp.

That we could just wrap up our camp and float down-river till we found a new one seemed to me amazing and miraculous. We could do this day after day until we reached the lower vehicle. If the river didn't do us in, it would be our greatest ally.

That second day, under the bright October sun, the river seemed to shrink to its real size, or perhaps its hazards were more visible and I had learned better how to stay out of trouble. I found myself rowing (with one gray palm) along a swirling, tumbling stream that seemed more mischievous than treacherous. We found a sub-alpine meadow and decided to pull out and camp there. We cooked our first hot meal—sausages on a blackened grill, canned corn niblets heated in a pot, and spuds in foil tossed into the coals. The sun sank early, and the frosty air moved in, but this time we were ready for the cold.

If my memory serves me, on the following morning, Scott and I set out to check the edges of the meadow for elk scat. We walked the perimeter together and returned to our camp by crossing the river in our rubber boots. Our tent was set back about fifty yards from the river, and we had to walk up a small, steep grade to see it. But what we saw was a huge bull moose with its nose to the entrance of our tent.

Perhaps we had approached him downwind, and no doubt the roar of the stream had disguised the sound of our rubber boots on the gravel. We watched as the moose circled and smelled our dwelling, curious as a cat. He was bigger and much older than the bull moose of the previous evening. He had one of those trophy heads you see on the cover of men's sporting journals—moose on the ground, hunter's boot on moose's head, rifle cradled, sleepy grin.

At last this old warrior moved away from our tent and up through the meadow. His antlers seemed almost too heavy to carry. He was ambling meditatively, as though wondering what aliens had landed in his favorite feeding grounds. The next time we looked around, he had circled us and wandered up into the trees, where he was gazing down at us like the moose of the previous evening. He stayed there for a long time.

We looked all over for signs of elk and found only old scat and old tracks. Down by the river, however, close to our camp, we found the enormous track of a grizzly, quite a fresh imprint, and that was enough to send us down the river once again.

AFTER NO MORE than two hours of running the Wild Hay, we found another meadow with a great deal of muskeg on one side and some sparse, dry woods on the other. When we had set up camp, Scott suggested that we split up. He would cross the river, skirt the muskeg, and explore the ridge beyond, where the grass looked sumptuous. Wild hay, I guess you'd call it. I would explore the wooded side and look for fresh scat.

It was a beautiful cool day. I trudged through groves of larch, alpine fir, and willows and discovered that my side of the river was pretty barren as far as elk browse went. So, in my rubber boots, I too crossed the river. It was a perfect crossing. No pools or deep water of any kind. Just a few inches of stream flowing over solid gravel. I wanted to see what lay beyond the muskeg. Scott's trail would eventually take him downstream, so mine took me upstream. I trudged along, finding, as usual, some old elk sign and some not-so-old moose sign and returned to within about a hundred yards of where I had crossed the river. This time I glassed the area around our tent to see if some critter was checking us out.

And yes, here we go again: a cow moose this time. She was feeding on the far shore scarcely a two-minute walk from our tent. I moved in closer for a better look. On my side of the river, her calf was also feeding. The cow looked my way and then continued to feed. The calf looked my way as well. It was about six months old, its fur a lighter brown than its mother's. It was long legged and gangly and stood more than three feet at the shoulder. As its mother had done, it turned away and continued to feed.

I assume to this day that these two animals had never seen a human before. There were no trappers' cabins in the area, no sign of horses. Scott and I had not even seen a human footprint in the Wild Hay valley. Moose are wary creatures, but clearly, on this warm afternoon, they had felt no threat from the aliens that trudged around on two legs.

I moved away from the calf and behind it, putting some trees between us. I had spotted the shallows where I could cross the creek and get to our tent without coming too close to the cow. I skirted the trees and went down to the creek, and there was the calf, perhaps three yards in front of me; it must have wandered over. It seemed to realize that I was merely attempting to cross the creek. I peeked through the branches of the nearest pine and saw the mother. She was looking my way, but then she went back to her browsing. I walked as if to go past the feeding calf, put my rifle in my left hand, and reached over and touched the calf on the back.

I DON'T REMEMBER why I had needed to get to our tent or whether I even crossed the stream. I think I might have reversed directions and walked away from the stream and the two feeding moose. I remember going around the muskeg and heading toward the grassy ridge where Scott was hunting. There was a beaver dam on a small stream, which had formed a nice wide pond. I stopped and sat down and cradled my rifle in my lap. I stared at the beaver house at the far end of the pond and eventually at the back-and-forth gliding of a beaver. I stared at the birds that flew overhead and at the sharp reflections on the pond and the deep woods beyond. *This is the Forest Primeval.* I have never been fond of highfalutin language, but these words seemed to wobble out of me because, with my right hand, I had just reached out and touched a moose calf on the back. Perhaps I had left a minuscule smudge of aluminum for the calf to carry away.

I gazed for a long time at the beaver pond, trying to think like a hunter. Here I am, perhaps fifteen miles from the nearest road, armed to the teeth, unafraid of bears or anything and thrilled as I can be. No, no, that wasn't it.

As a writer who used to hunt, I feel some obligation to my readers to discharge this old rifle at something. A legal bull elk or an illegal bull moose or perhaps a marauding wolf. But this is the climax of my great adventure: staring at a beaver pond and thinking about a moose calf that I touched. Staring at beavers and birds and hypnotized by wilderness and solitude, and feeling as connected to a wild place as I had ever felt. The moment did not stretch out for very long, maybe half an hour. Words like *happiness* or *contentment* or *clarity of mind* or *forest primeval* don't even get me halfway. It's hard to paint a scene when you're part of the picture, and for the first time in my life, in all that solitude, I had become part of the picture.

We counted seventeen moose on that trip. The last two were another cow and her calf, these ones only a mile or so from a bridge, a campground, and a ranger tower that would mark the end of our trip and the return of the road where one of our cars was parked. When the cow spotted us, she and her calf ran for the woods. The cow was loping away on three legs and doing an admirable job of it. One of her hind legs swung uselessly by her side, perhaps a casualty from a hunter's bullet. I will never forget the contrast between these wary campground moose and the placid, curious creatures we had seen in the deeper wilderness, those great innocents who presided over a perfect world.

THERE IS A bar in New York City where young men gather wearing red mackinaw shirts, hunting boots, camouflage pants, and hunting jackets. Others wear business suits. This is the Black Bear Lodge on Third Avenue in Gramercy Park. These men come here in impressive numbers to play a video game known as *Big Buck Hunter Pro*. There are only two hunting machines, so the lineups are very long. They play the game by grabbing a shotgun and firing at moose and elk and other animals on screen, and their trophy animals die electronically. The manager of the bar, Belle Caplis, describes young men in business suits who "untuck their shirts and fire away." Cabela, the corporate fashion-conscious outfitter, has sold more than thirteen million copies of such games as *Dangerous Hunts 2009* and *Legendary Adventures*.

A burgeoning culture of high-tech hunters is spreading throughout North America and beyond. Some people (I won't call them hunters) play a game where they can line up a live, captive animal with their cursor, which guides a remote-controlled gun located in some far-off country, and kill the animal by clicking their mouse. Aren't computers wonderful?

I tease myself with the fantasy that some of these cyber-hunters—perhaps the ones who are not yet hard-core—might read this chapter, measure the appalling gulf between my experience on the Wild Hay River and their own in one of the many sports bars across North America, be jolted into a profound awakening, and go and sin no more. Or at least find some woods and take a walk.

More and more this is the bewildering culture that I am addressing. Less and less do I find people who have lived the experience of going out into the wilderness and coming back with that healthy glow, those calloused paddle fingers (and perhaps gray palms), the clothes that smell of campfires and pine sap, and those wonderful stories about the moose that got away.

When my wife, Honor, and I take our walks into the coulees near Saskatoon (population 210,000) in the wintertime, we are often alone. When we fish the trout ponds with our friends up on the Hanson Lake Road, we are alone. When my hunting buddy Doug Elsasser walks the community pasture and meadows of the Assiniboine Valley for whitetails, he is alone. When we canoe the South Saskatchewan River with our friends from Van-couver, we are once more all alone. In the culture that surrounds me, the people explore websites and new res-taurants and the farmers' market, and if they are lucky, they explore the beaches of Cuba and Mexico when the weather gets cold. The people of this culture explore malls and shop in specialty clothing stores with names like The Outdoor Edge, The HOBO Shop, or The Forest Primeval. A walk in the woods has been largely replaced by a noisy and rapid excursion on an all-terrain vehicle or a snowmobile.

I am sounding like an old fart, bristling with disapproval. In some circles these days, I would be as welcome at a party as Edgar Allan Poe's raven.

Or maybe the Ancient Mariner: *Hi, I'm Dave Carpenter. Would you be my wedding guest? Good, because I have seen such things, I have had a vision of the perfect world, I have touched a live moose in the wild. Oh, ye who have touched a live moose may cast the first stone.*

Enough of my personal resentments. Let's look at how people regarded hunting during this same time when recreational hunting was (still, just barely) thought to be a salutary, even soul-restoring adventure. It's *Zeitgeist* time at the old corral.

## 4 THE DAWNING OF AMBIVALENCE

*I must admit to not being the most patient person in a deer stand*
*but if I know that a big buck is utilizing the area, I sure get a lot more*
*patient. I'd say that trail cameras are without question the most*
*significant tool to come along for the trophy deer hunter in the past few*
*decades. Most of the battle with hunting trophy deer is hunting*
*where they are. With the camera, there is no doubt where they are.*
T.J. SCHWANKY, "Trail Cameras," *The Outdoor Edge*, Vol.17, Issue 1

*I avoid hook-and-bullet magazines, which put me off with*
*their photos of bows that look like missile launchers and*
*weird-shaped rifles with ever larger scopes and ever more deadly*
*loads. They promote technological prowess far above knowledge*
*of animals or skill in the outdoors. And they focus on killing.*
*They show animals with cross-hairs super-imposed, or sprawled with*
*unshaven men hunched over them—a friend calls this horn porn.*
*And it is. What it urges is that the act of possession is supreme.*
C.L. RAWLINS, "I Like to Talk about Animals," *A Hunter's Heart*

AMBIVALENCE IS doublemindedness toward some thing, mixed feelings. The opposite of ambivalence is singlemindedness. Growing up in an oil-rich province in the west end of Edmonton in the 1950s, I thought it was a good thing to be singleminded. All the neat guys in my neighborhood were singleminded. None of my friends used the word *ambivalent*. Nor did any of my older brother's friends use this word—*and they read books*. Singleminded, though: there was a word for you. Shane was singleminded when he shot every guy in the bar at the end of the movie. The soldiers who conquered Hitler's armies—at least the ones in the movies before Marlon Brando's time—they were all singleminded. The word *singleminded* went with such resolute words as *pursuit* and *conquest* and *resolve*.

In 1959, when Dad gave me a shotgun for my birthday, I pursued grouse and ducks with singleminded fervor.

Quite possibly I never heard the word *ambivalence* uttered until the early 1960s, when I was a university student. This was about the time when Jack Lemmon starred in *The Apartment* with Shirley MacLaine. If ever there was a movie actor with a capacity for ambivalence, Jack Lemmon was it. But it was Henry Kreisel, my English prof, who first used this word in my presence. He used it in connection with psychoanalysis, literature, emotional states, the *Zeitgeist* of the twentieth century.

Ambivalence was still a hard sell at home. It wasn't a good word to take to the supper table. My brother was studying chemical engineering, and he had little use for ambivalence. My father was a broker, and in the stock market, he who hesitated was lost. Ambivalence was probably bad for business. My mother had a no-nonsense attitude to getting her boys up in the morning and off to classes. If you wanted to explore your ambivalence to your studies, do it in the summer.

For years in the 1950s and early 1960s, I read a lot of hunting literature. I could have divided it all into ambivalent or singleminded literature, but I didn't because I loved all of it. The magazine *Outdoor Life* was as singleminded as anyone in my family. You got the right equipment, you learned the right techniques, you found your deer, you lined it up, you squeezed the trigger. You smiled around your pipe with singleminded pride at what you had accomplished.

The ad for Gillette Blue Blades was an anthem of singlemindedness: "Look sharp, feel sharp, be sharp!"

One way of reconstructing the spirit of this time, of course, is to ransack the memory, as I have already done in this book. But memory being what it is (a narrator that arranges the facts in order to recount them by the fireside), we need historical benchmarks to keep us honest. For me, these benchmarks are the books I read about hunting from the mid-1950s to the end of the 1960s. I still have copies of William Faulkner's *Go Down, Moses*, Ernest Hemingway's *Green Hills of Africa*, *Measure of the Year* by Roderick Haig-Brown, and *The Treasury of Hunting* by Larry Koller. I am not going to bother with the usual distinctions between fiction and nonfiction here, because what really interests me is the attitudes toward hunting embedded in the books.

I have a beautiful hardback edition of Koller's book. It lies on my bookshelf at least a foot to the right of Hemingway's works. Like Teddy Roosevelt, Koller writes with boundless enthusiasm about all aspects of hunting in North America, and his knowledge of guns old and new is encyclopedic. But unlike Roosevelt, who frequently hunted out West simply to provide meat for his wranglers, Larry Koller posits a hierarchy of hunters, with the meat hunter on the low end and the trophy hunter up on high. Koller professes great respect for the alpha predators (grizzlies and their bigger cousins, the Alaskan browns) and antlered animals (especially deer and elk). In fact, most animals that have been reified by the hunting fraternity and made into trophies are worthy of his respect.

Again, like Roosevelt, Koller saves his contempt for what he and my contemporaries called varmints (derived from the word *vermin*): cougars, bobcats, black bears, raptors, and many other creatures that are not usually considered good to eat. Varmints, he says, "are suitable victims for the hunter, whether his armament is rim-fire or center-fire rifle, shotgun, or handgun." Varmints were like the shmoos in *Li'l Abner,* I suppose—the gift that keeps on giving. They provide a hunter with live targets "to develop his stalking and shooting skill." Koller likens this assortment of varmints to "a shooting laboratory" for the "development of new cartridges and new loads in standard calibers."

A black bear, to Larry Koller, is really just "an innocuous clown." You can bait the bear with garbage or a dead horse, run it with dogs, trap the bear, or smoke it out of the den "if you want one badly enough—but none of this makes him a real game animal."

Mountain lions are "cowardly." Their appeal for Koller is apparently to "provide some hair-raising kicks for hound-dog varmint hunters." According to Koller's survey, none of which he includes in his book, of the thousands of these big cats that have been killed or captured by hunting parties in mid-century America, "only a scattered half dozen" have fought back. When treed, the cougar "snarls viciously, belying his true cowardly nature."

Hawks can be "decoyed to a mounted owl just as readily as crows, and provide even faster shotgun work." Golden eagles are apparently as heinous as varmints can get—the wildlife equivalent of serial killers. These predators compete with hunters for wild game by killing young sheep, goats, antelope, and fawns, and apparently they prey heavily on livestock. I did not know this, and I am left a little breathless with an image of eagles carrying off lambs and slaughtering calves. Very little of this predation shows up in the bird books, but we are assured in Koller's irrepressible voice that "as long as the golden eagle lives in big-game country," this predation will continue.

Ah, but help is at hand. A game-warden friend of Koller's in eastern Montana has been fighting eagles for many years. At last count, the warden's score on these great birds was something over three thousand! Koller expressed little doubt that the excellence of the antelope and mule-deer hunting in his buddy's territory is much improved owing to the warden's skill with a .243 Winchester.

Koller was the quintessence of singlemindedness.

He reminds us, for example, that the mountain grizzly is one of the rarest prizes among the whole range of North American trophies. For hunters who don't have a lot of time to go stomping through the woods, the grizzly is killed by baiting more often than not. This method, according to Koller, does not rate very high as sport, but if success is what you're after, it is the only way to fly. Koller has to admit, however, that there is no good grizzly hunting to be had in the lower forty-eight states.

Note the order of his observations: (1) single out the endangered species; (2) show us how to kill it; (3) lament the absence of said species. This is Koller's pattern throughout *The Treasury of Hunting*. He cautions his readers against killing certain endangered species, then demonstrates the most efficient way to do it. His conclusion to this spectacle of loss, from the vanishing grizzlies to the sage grouse and pinnated grouse, passenger pigeons, New England heath hens, great auks, Labrador ducks, and so on usually has something to do with fate. The moose in New England "gradually disappeared under the pressure of progress." Progress is better roads, bigger towns and cities, and, of course, more efficient rifles.

I would like to think that Koller is unique among outdoor journalists in his ability to shrug off responsibility for vanishing wildlife, for his tendency to ascribe contrasting moral qualities to the animals for which he has contempt and the ones he admires, and for the ease with which he reduces fascinating and beautiful animals to mere targets. But readers of outdoor magazines everywhere in North America will already know that Larry Koller has not cornered the market on indifference to the plight of the animals he kills.

We are talking about an entire culture here. As a hunter in my twenties, I admired Koller's book. Lots of guys admired this book. We must have grown up thinking that the animals were there for our shooting pleasure. Just as farm animals were there simply to feed us, the animals in the wilderness were a *resource*.

Where does this attitude come from that puts us at the top of a moral hierarchy? I will never know for sure, but sometimes I think it's as old as Genesis 1, verse 28: "God blessed [man and woman], and God said to them, 'Be fruitful and multiply, and fill the earth and subdue it; and have dominion over the fish of the sea and over the birds of the air and over every living thing that moves upon the earth.' " When we think about the kind of heartless entitlement that passage has inspired, the subjugation of all that is wild, and the domestication of the land and its creatures and the people who hunted them, Genesis reads like a farmer's dream and a hunter's nightmare.

If God or King James had hired *me* to write this passage, I would have told the story as follows. *God blessed them and said to them, "Go forth and maintain a stable economy and a population based on sustainable growth. Go forth and subtract if you have to, and explore the earth and enjoy it; and live in harmony with the fish of the sea and the* birds of the air, and don't just shoot the birds because some doofus in a hunting magazine told you they were mere targets that didn't feel pain."

What happens when we come to believe that animals are subjects of our dominion, merely there for our needs and not there in and for themselves, cohabitants of the planet, so to speak, is that we objectify them without the tiniest regret. Instead of prairies and forests, we end up with industrial space in which wild flora are labeled *weeds*. And the wild animals become targets. Who could possibly lament the destruction of a mere target?

Surely not Ernest Hemingway. During my coming of age, he was a hero to all of us who loved the out-of-doors, the embodiment of courage, manliness, and passion for the hunt. Skillful as Larry Koller was at writing about guns, he was incapable of writing about wild animals. Koller could never have written the following description of a fallen kudu bull: "I looked at him, big, long-legged, a smooth gray with the white stripes and the great, curling, sweeping horns, brown as walnut meats, and ivory pointed, at the big ears and the great, lovely heavy-maned neck the white chevron between his eyes and the white of his muzzle and I stooped over and touched him to try to believe it. He was lying on the side where the bullet had gone in and there was not a mark on him and he smelled sweet and lovely like the breath of cattle and the odor of thyme after rain."

This description is from Hemingway's *Green Hills of Africa*, a nonfiction account of his safari in December 1933. What strikes me in this description is the intimacy and respect that Hemingway demonstrates toward the animal he has just brought down. He stoops over to touch the great beast "to try to believe it" and smells an odor that rises like the soul of a dying saint.

Teddy Roosevelt was Ernest Hemingway's first and greatest hero. And very much like Roosevelt would have done, Hemingway argues strenuously against baiting and shooting lions from blinds and shooting them from vehicles. He calls it "murder." He rails against hunters who shoot pronghorn antelope from jeeps. He writes of dangerous trophy animals like the African buffalo and the leopard with great respect.

The following description of Hemingway shooting hyenas, then, reads like a curious exception to the rule. "Highly humorous was the hyena obscenely loping, full belly dragging, at daylight on the plain, who, shot from the stern, skittered on into speed to tumble end over end. Mirth provoking was the hyena that stopped out of range by an alkali lake to look back and, hit in the chest, went over on his back, his four feet and his full belly in the air. Nothing could be more jolly than the hyena coming suddenly wedge-headed and stinking out of high grass by a *donga*, hit at ten yards, who raced his tail in three narrowing, scampering circles until he died."

Hemingway's gun-bearer M'Cola finds this all very funny, but Hemingway seems to share in the joke. He is the shooter here. Note his summary of animals killed during his first week or two in Africa. It is worthy of Teddy Roosevelt at his most rapacious. "As far as bag goes, if anyone is interested, we have good heads of Eland, Waterbuck, Grant Robertsi and other gazelles. A fine roan antelope, two big leopard, and excellent, if

not record, impala; also the limit all around on cheetah.
They are much too nice an animal to shoot and I will
never kill another . . . On the other hand we shot thirty-
five hyena out of the lot that follow the wildebeeste
migration to keep after the cows that are about to calve
and wish we had ammunition to kill a hundred."

Sharks fare no better in Hemingway's sights. Again,
note the careful accounting of the dead. "I have a
Thompson Sub Machine gun and we shoot sharks with
it. Shot 27 in two weeks. All over ten feet long. As soon
as they put their heads out we give them a burst."

I have a wary admiration for Hemingway's respect
for the animals he kills, but it's difficult to separate
my cherished version of him as a writer from the man
who created such carnage. The wildlife, like his many
wives, seem to be there solely for his pleasure, however
ill-conceived. Of game birds, he confesses: "I think they
all were made to shoot because if they were not why
did they give them that whirr of wings that moves you
suddenly more than any love of country? Why did they
make them all so good to eat and why did they make the
ones with silent flight like wood-cock, snipe, and lesser
bustard, better eating even than the rest?" No doubt this
is an example of Hemingway humor, but I can't quite
escape the suspicion that he means every word of it.

Which leads me to the ultimate puzzle: Hemingway's
churning compulsion to kill wild game. He writes about
it with characteristic candor in *Death in the Afternoon*.
"One of the greatest pleasures . . . is the feeling of rebellion against death which comes from its administering.
Once you accept the rule of death, thou shalt not kill

is an easily and naturally obeyed commandment. But when a man is still in rebellion against death he has a pleasure in taking to himself one of the Godlike attributes; that of giving it. This is one of the most profound feelings in those men who enjoy killing."

This impulse in Hemingway—killing to cheat death, killing to keep alive—resurfaces elsewhere in his writing. Harry, the dying protagonist of Hemingway's classic short story "The Snows of Kilimanjaro," is an obvious projection of the Hemingway persona: he is obsessed with manliness, he loves to hunt in Africa, and he is a talented writer who marries wealthy women whom he accuses of distracting him from his writing. Harry is dying of gangrene poisoning in his leg. He and his wife sit beneath the shade of a great mimosa tree, waiting for a rescue plane to arrive, and Harry lapses into a wounding tirade against his wife. She begins to weep. When he observes the damage he has done, he says, "Listen . . . do you think that it is fun to do this? I don't know why I'm doing it. It's trying to kill to keep yourself alive."

Perhaps the ambivalence we all manifest is unique, our own brand of mixed feelings. If so, Hemingway's ambivalence about hunting is as vexed and doubleminded as it comes. In a life dogged with limited achievement, uncertainty, and doubt, I prefer my own brand of ambivalence.

WILLIAM FAULKNER'S BOOKS sit to the left of Hemingway's on the shelf of my study. On the surface of things, Faulkner matches up rather nicely with Hemingway. They were born and died in the same era, only a few years apart at both ends. They were both superb novelists, both Nobel Laureates, and both chronic drinkers. Like Hemingway, Faulkner was a passionate hunter, and he kept at it all his life, but in his late fifties, unlike Hemingway, Faulkner found himself mellowing in unexpected ways. In a letter to Jean Stein, he said that he was about to return to the Delta country in Mississippi for his annual November hunt. He tells her, however, that he no longer wanted to shoot any deer. He simply wanted to chase them on his horse. His confession went farther. He told her that he did not want to kill anything anymore and that he would probably give his guns away. Every time he saw a wild animal that, ordinarily, he and his friends would try to hunt down, he felt loath to pull the trigger. He was returning to the Delta for the companionship with his old friends and the whiskey and the stories around the campfire. When Faulkner moved to Virginia at the end of his life, he continued to pursue the fox hunt, but like many of his companions, he had no interest in killing a fox.

In my hunting prime, I read Faulkner like scripture. The most profound—the greatest—hunting story I have ever been able to find is Faulkner's "The Bear," a novella of some 132 pages. It was published in a linked sequence of Faulkner stories entitled *Go Down, Moses* (1942). In "The Bear," young Ike McCaslin is on a quest to hunt for Old Ben, a huge black bear with a trap-ruined foot, a quarry that had become larger than life in the Delta country of rural Mississippi. Old Ben was the scourge of countless farmers in Yoknapatawpha County, Faulkner's mythical kingdom. The bear had a reputation for invading farms and making off with a wide assortment of animals. Many hunters came to the Big Woods to kill him, but Old Ben simply mangled their dogs and somehow absorbed all the ammunition they could fire at him. The bear had entered the young Ike McCaslin's imagination the way monsters inhabit our dreams, but this monster seems to have inspired more awe than terror in Ike's mind. Gradually the bear becomes godlike.

When the story begins, Ike is sixteen years old and already a skilled hunter and woodsman. His mentor has been Sam Fathers, the son of a Chickasaw chief and a black slave woman. Ike's most memorable hunting companion is Boon Hogganbeck, a sort of likeable troglodyte who is also part Chickasaw. Ike is aching to see the bear, even for an instant, but he has no luck until he starts to confer with Sam Fathers.

Sam tells him that his rifle is the problem, that Ike will have to choose between carrying his rifle into the woods and seeing the bear. As long as young Ike carries a weapon in his quest to see the bear, he is tainted and the bear will not show itself. Ike's reliance on his rifle, and on the manmade technology the rifle represents, seems to militate against the strange natural powers that reign in the forest. Unarmed, Ike returns to the woods, relying only upon his watch and compass to orient himself, but leaving the rifle behind is clearly not enough. He has to relinquish completely to the unseen powers of the forest. He offers up his watch and compass by hanging them on the branches of a bush. Thus stripped of all his manmade acoutrements, young Ike can enter the woods.

Soon he is lost, but he fights down the panic and spies a crooked print in the ground, and another one, and another. The prints lead him right back to his abandoned watch, and compass, and then he sees the bear: "It did not emerge, appear: it was just there, immobile, fixed in the green and windless noon's hot dappling, not as big as he had dreamed it but as big as he had expected, bigger, dimensionless against the dappled obscurity, looking at him." Note how lyrical Faulkner's prose has become. The "dimensionless" bear is presented to us as though it were a ghost, a mythic presence, something more than a wild creature. The bear leaves the scene as mysteriously as it arrived. It doesn't amble back into the forest. "It faded, sank back into the wilderness without motion." Again, there is more awe than fear evoked by Ike's brief sighting of the bear.

The climax of the story comes when the bear is at last cornered by an unholy tribe of dogs and hunters. This final confrontation between the bear and its pursuers, though presented in realistic detail, reads like a saga from southern folklore. Something mightier than a bear is killed in this scene, and Ike McCaslin is left to contemplate the end of an era, the death of a god.

Oddly enough, however, this fine story does not end with the death of the bear. It goes on in its moody, obscure, and brilliant way for at least seventy more pages. The bear is gone, but a strange momentum carries us along with Ike and his compatriots through a bewildering process of introspection and grieving. When the bear dies, so does Sam Fathers and his demonic dog. Without the bear and old Sam to preside over the Big Woods, the wilderness is bereft and unguarded, and it is doomed to fall prey to the sawmills and timber crews that will be nibbling at the edges of the great forest. Before the lumber company moves in to cut the remaining timber, however, Ike returns to walk the woods again, this time as a young man. He seeks out his old hunting companion, Boon Hogganbeck, who is apparently hunting near an old gum tree that all the hunters use as a reconnoitering place.

Boon was the man who ultimately slew the bear. He was a huge powerful clumsy fellow who was as fearless and faithful as any hunting dog, and almost as smart. But like Old Ben the bear, Boon was destined to become a legend, a Daniel Boone without the woodsy wisdom, the woodcraft, or the glamor.

Before Ike can find Boon at the old gum tree, he wanders through the bearless woods lost in thought and almost steps on an old rattler. The snake is over six feet long, and presented to us in realistic terms, but it is interesting how Faulkner's mythic imagery gathers around this creature in the same way that it gave depth to the bear. The head of the rattlesnake is raised higher than Ike's knee and within easy striking distance of Ike. The snake is described as old, its markings as dull as the leafless woods in spring where, "it crawled and lurked: the old one, the ancient and accursed about the earth, fatal and solitary."

This is not just an eastern diamondback rattler, the largest and most dangerous of all North American venomous snakes, but "the old one, the ancient and accursed

about the earth." To Ike, this is the same serpent, "evoca-
tive of all knowledge," that promised ultimate wisdom
to Eve in that other garden where it all began. Perhaps
he sees the serpent as the new landlord of this hunter's
paradise. The bear has been replaced by a new god, one
that will preside over the dismantling of the Big Woods.
It glides away, and Ike recovers and walks on.

He continues to search for Boon until he hears a
frenzied hammering noise coming from the direction
of the gum tree. This tree is full of squirrels in a sudden state of panic. Several dozen of them are scurrying
all over the tree from twig to branch as though they
had been ambushed. The noise Ike had heard was Boon
hammering away at the breech of his old dismembered
gun, trying to repair it, as though he had gone insane.
Remember, this is Boon Hogganbeck, the ultimate bear
slayer, who has caught the stranded squirrels by surprise.
He doesn't look up at Ike's approach; he simply yells at
him to get out of his way. The squirrels are Boon's for the
killing.

Like *Moby Dick*, this is a hunting story, and like *Moby
Dick*, Faulkner's tale is a great deal more. He is not going
to lead us to the heart of the Big Woods just to watch
a great bear get run down and killed. He is going to
look long and hard at the consequences of this act, the
inevitable destruction of the bear's habitat and, with it,
the loss of that heroic world of great hunters and near-
mythic beasts. Not that hunting is inherently wrong, but
man's heartless presumption that he can own the wilderness and turn it into a quick profit, this destruction and
consequent loss of paradise becomes a tragedy of biblical

proportions. This conclusion seems entirely consistent with the views of a writer who is losing his instinct for the kill. But Faulkner's ambivalence toward hunting has allowed him to create a monument of sad wisdom, which is his tribute to the doomed wilderness.

HAIG-BROWN, RODERICK, LIES to the left of Hemingway, Ernest, on my shelf. Moving from the work of Hemingway and Faulkner to the writings of Roderick Haig-Brown is like choosing a hunting buddy who is closer to home, less neurotically driven, and perhaps not so morose to drink with. His politics were decidedly to the left of those of Teddy Roosevelt. Haig-Brown was to British Columbia as his contemporary Aldo Leopold was to Wisconsin. From my youthful reading days to my late twenties, I found no one who wrote about fishing and hunting with greater authority than Roderick Haig-Brown. Naturalist, magistrate, fly-fisher, hunter, bureaucrat, and above all, a writer, he penned novels and dabbled in poetry, but he became famous primarily from his nature writing in *Life,* the *New Yorker, Harper's,* the *Atlantic Monthly,* and *Outdoor Life* and with such nonfiction books as *A River Never Sleeps* and *Measure of the Year.*

As a young émigré in Campbell River, British Columbia, Haig-Brown attempted to earn a living as a writer. He acquired a fascination with mountain lions, so he apprenticed himself to a famed hunter on Vancouver Island, John Cecil "Cougar" Smith. Although his mentor claimed to have killed at least six hundred cougars in his career as a bounty hunter, Haig-Brown apparently lost heart for the kill after taking his first two or three cougars. In his youth, he was a prodigious killer of game birds, rabbits, and deer, but with these great cats that fascinated him so, he came to "hate the moment of the shot."

I wonder what Larry Koller would have said about Roderick Haig-Brown? *Hmm. Sounds a bit doubleminded to me.*

Cougar hunting, Haig-Brown claims, is "immeasurably the most interesting form of large-game hunting I have ever known, the strongest test of a man's woodcraft and endurance, calling for truly beautiful work by well-trained dogs . . . ," but cougar killing clearly went against his grain. His early novel *Panther* was written almost entirely from the point of view of the cougar, and from this narration we gain a surprisingly intimate view of the life cycle of the great cats: their growth to maturity, their hunting patterns, their rutting, the enemies they had to contend with, their legendary curiosity.

In *Measure of the Year* (1950), Haig-Brown recounts stories of heedless slaughter around Campbell River and elsewhere and predicts that the outcome will be sad indeed for the most vulnerable of wild creatures: the ivory-billed woodpecker, for example, and the trumpeter swan. He tells a particularly heartbreaking story of two men with rifles and a speedboat who shoot a swan, wound it, chase it down with their boat, and kill it.

Remember the thousands upon thousands of hunters to whom hunting is shooting and everything between shots is slow. Remember how many men believe that a bag limit, preferably in competition with their fellows, is high triumph. Remember the hunters who overshoot limits, who fail to pick up birds they have killed and shoot others instead, who wound more birds than they ever bring home. Remember that the number and proportion of all these increases steadily year by year, that new roads open up new country, that settlement and development closes old country, and I think the pattern is clear. There cannot be stocks of wild life to maintain the sport indefinitely.

Heartless hunting, then, is the enemy, and compassionate hunting is the answer for Haig-Brown and his many disciples. In this way, he can argue that hunters are the

keenest and most effective of all conservationists. If they are responsible for nine-tenths of the avoidable destruction of wildlife, they are responsible for at least nine-tenths of the effective conservation, because they have the numbers and organization and voting weight to be effective, and because they have the strongest of all possible reasons to be effective: their own survival as hunters is exactly related to the survival of the creatures they hunt . . . The hardest task they have to do is to persuade their fellow hunters that sport is hunting, not killing.

In an era when environmentalism had not yet become a word, Haig-Brown became the prototype of the hunter-as-environmentalist, the hunter with a conscience. He is one of those writers, like Faulkner and Hemingway, who entered my bloodstream and never quite left it. There are moments in my writing life when I wonder if I've plagiarized him. There have been moments in my hunting life when he might almost have guided me. The following tale describes one such moment.

SCOTT SMITH AND I attempted once again to run the Wild Hay River, he in his canoe and I once more in my rubber dinghy and nonmatching oars. But this time hunting was to prove impossible; the river had fallen drastically, and it was now too shallow for us to run it. Right then and there, we had to make a decision. Scott had a girlfriend in Edmonton, and I did not, so with some reluctance, he drove back to Edmonton, leaving me and my Volkswagen Beetle to my own devices.

It was a stunningly beautiful morning in early October. I had brought my fly rod along just in case. Scott reminded me that I was a mere hour's drive from a lake in Jasper that we had often fished in the fall. Mina Lake. It was full of brook trout. During the previous fall I had seen an enormous one nosing through the shallows. I promised that brookie I'd be back for another engagement. And now, if I had timed things right, these brookies would be staging in their prespawning mode. They would become territorial and aggressive and race each other to get to a fly. Driving to Jasper was an easy decision.

Because it was late in the year, if my memory serves me, there was no one manning the gate at the park entrance. And there was certainly no sign of any conservation officers. There were no tourists left to bother about. I drove north of the Jasper townsite on the Pyramid Lake Road and parked at the Mina Lake trailhead.

I had my rifle in the car. The area was deserted. I had heard some reports of lowland grizzlies on this trail, and although I'd never seen one, I had seen several black bears here. Knowing that I would be all alone on the trail with nothing but a fly rod to protect me—well, that made me nervous enough to reconsider the whole excursion. But I wanted to have a go at those lovely brook trout.

Now, here's a real confession. I loaded my rifle and threw it over my shoulder. On a hike in the mountain parks, or any other wildlife preserve, this is a really stupid thing to do. Honestly, I never want to be that young again.

The fly-fishing was splendid that day. I caught and released at least a dozen brook trout and kept two nice ones. I would use these fish to feed my friends who were hosting me that night at a cabin. I cleaned the two fish and tossed the guts to some mink that were foraging among some rock ledges by the side of the lake. An angler more mindful than I on that day would have buried the guts, but these mink were clearly hungry for them, so I broke one of the rules of prudent fishing. I guess it was a day for breaking rules.

I think my rifle was again strapped over my shoulder, my fly rod was in my right hand, and with the other I must have carried the fish on a stick that I would have thrust through their gills and out the jaws. In other words, my hands were full and I smelled of fish. I had a basketball referee's whistle on a lanyard around my neck. In those days, in case of danger from a bear or in case of getting lost, we carried loud whistles.

The hike to my car was about three miles. The trail takes you down from Mina through the forest to a small parking lot at the side of the Pyramid Lake Road. These are lowland mountains, not at all like the towering mountains in Yoho or Lake Louise, and so about half the trees along the trail are deciduous, and in early October the drying yellow leaves of aspens absolutely covered the ground. You could not walk quietly along the path; you would be shuffling and crunching leaves as you went.

I had gone about a mile down the trail when I heard, from a ridge above me, a deer, or some animal, prancing through the trees. I could only just make it out as it descended through the recently bare aspens and wild berry bushes. As I continued along the trail, the noise from this deer became louder, and I remember thinking that *wild animals were supposed to be stealthy movers.* But the crisp fallen leaves would not allow my friend the deer to approach quietly, and I kept on walking, no doubt wrapped in a dream of stuffed and baked brook trout.

And then I stopped walking and squinted through the aspens and dogwood at the lovely fawn-colored creature that approached me. It was the *approaching* part that gave me pause. It was now about a hundred feet away. I raised the whistle to my lips and gave it a mighty blast. The deer seemed to deflate and disappear by crouching down behind some berry bushes.

Even a clueless young guy, if he's done any camping and hiking, knows a few things about deer. They don't tend to follow people in the bush, and when they have been whistled at, they don't crouch down behind the shrubbery to remain out of sight. If they are even the slightest bit alarmed, they bound away through the trees. This particular deer had a very long tail with a black tip, and although the deer in question was out of sight, its tail swayed back and forth above the bushes like a cobra to the music of a flute.

*Oh, Jesus, it wasn't a deer.*

I had not intended to troll for cougars that day, but I'd found one. I backed away and continued down the trail, thinking that my whistle had done its work. But the cougar followed me, and by the time I had reached the halfway point on the trail, it was less than fifty feet from me, crouched down in the open now, an appallingly beautiful big cat.

Until this moment, I had probably forgotten that I had a loaded rifle hanging from my shoulder. I lowered the fish and my fly rod and took the rifle into both hands. I did not raise the rifle to aim it or even lever a shell into the breech. I simply stared at the cat, and it stared right back at me. The air from Mina Lake to this point on the trail must have been saturated with the aroma of trout guts. And here was the result of my carelessness.

I might have stood there on the trail gawking at the cougar for a minute or more. I remember it as a fairly long time. And I will never prove this to anyone, but it seems to me that something passed between me and the great cat—a message of some kind: that I now knew what it was, and that it had stalked me, and because of this thing I held with both hands in front of my chest, I was not afraid of it. I wanted to stay longer and stretch out the moment of our encounter, just as right now, as I write these words, I want to hang on to this moment and gaze back through forty years into those amazingly beautiful wild and terrible eyes.

But I had things to do, friends to share supper with. Besides, killing a cougar was unthinkable. I retrieved the stick with the two trout, picked up the fly rod, shouldered my rifle, and backed away down the path. At last I turned my back on the great cat and walked all the way to my car.

Not once during this encounter did I recall the words of Teddy Roosevelt, Larry Koller, Ernest Hemingway, William Faulkner, or Roderick Haig-Brown. Not once did I revisit the two versions of the cougar Koller and Haig-Brown had presented to me in their books. The cougar as spitting coward. The cougar as superb hunter and stalker. But I came to a moment of discovery there, that in using my rifle not as a weapon but merely as a thing to hold in reserve, something that allowed me enough repose to gaze upon the perfect beauty of a mountain lion, I was firmly in the camp of Haig-Brown and Faulkner. Without a moment's choosing, I had somehow chosen sides.

# 5 THROWBACKS

*Nimrod . . . was the first on earth to be a mighty*
*man. He was a mighty hunter before the Lord.*
GENESIS 10, *verses 8–9*

*The promoter of the colossal task [building the Tower of Babel,*
*which would reach up into the heavens] was Noah's grandson*
*Nimrod, whose mad ambition was to invade the Kingdom of God.*
ALBERTO MANGUEL, *The City of Words*

HUNTING IN the late sixties and early seventies, for me,
was somehow different from my earlier excursions.
It was like the switch from slow dance and jive to detached,
free-form rock 'n roll. In the fifties we held our partner or our
partner's hands; we tried to learn the moves and so did they.
But with sixties rock 'n roll, all conventions went out the door
as we gyrated our bodies farther and farther away from our
partners and from what our parents thought we should do.
Hunting in my youth derived entirely from what my dad and
his generation of hunters taught me. There were truths that

boys and men tended to accept, especially that hunting was far and away the best thing a dad could do with his kid.

Around the time I was stalked by the cougar in Jasper Park, however, something had begun to change. Hunting had become such a suspect form of recreation that people all around me seemed to pretend it didn't exist. Leaf through a thousand magazines of general interest (*Maclean's*, *Time*, *Life*, *People*, the *Atlantic Monthly*, etc.) during the mid-sixties to the early seventies, the chronicles of urban and rural life, you might look in vain for a single item on hunting. Hunting, from the dawning of the Age of Aquarius to the last toke of exhausted hippydom, was considered more anachronistic than girdles, hula hoops, and Guy Lombardo. Who knows? If you pursued this passion for guns and shooting, you might end up like Hemingway did.

My awareness of this cultural shift came slowly. It started when I moved to the United States to pursue a master's degree. I went off to Eugene, Oregon, in 1965 and eventually came to live in a ramshackle house with a fellow from Belfast named Jack Foster. Our landlord and lady were Bill and Peggy Roecker, a welcoming young couple who often invited us to join them in Thanksgiving dinners or parties downstairs or outings of all kinds. Bill Roecker (pronounced "wrecker") was a young writer who had just returned from his military service when the war in Vietnam was really heating up. He seemed very glad to be out of the army and back hitting the books. He was a promising writer and poet, a profane, burly fellow with a voice like an avalanche. "Carpenter, ya gotta see this! I just shot the shit outta this duck!" If Walt Whitman hadn't first conceived of the barbaric yawp, Roecker would have invented it. He would roar these words as a goad to my restrained Canadian ways. He took Jack and me hunting and fishing a number of times along the creeks and ridges of the Willamette Valley.

Bill had an ex-army buddy named Johnny Merwin who never seemed at home in the postmilitary world, except when he was hunting or fishing somewhere back in the hills. He was a wild man in every possible way. Wild when drunk, wild on the hunt, wild in courtship, wild as the animals. He could mimic the calls of geese, crows, herons, and songbirds or the snarls of cougars and bears. With his gangly body he could even mimic the movements of these critters. As we bounced along the trails in Roecker's camper, without warning, Johnny would start braying or squawking to a chorus of belly laughs. He seemed to prefer this exotic version of hee-haw to talking with us.

Roecker and Merwin. These were our hunting buddies, circa 1966, when that good old time became something else entirely. They were mighty and mad like Nimrod.

On campus, Hemingway's stock was falling. Our professor seemed compelled to defend his life and his work and his suicide to classrooms of skeptical readers. The bombing escalations in Vietnam had become increasingly unpopular. Anything to do with guns, in this nation stacked high with guns, became suspect. Guns were what the National Guard and the police carried in their attempts to restrain protesters, evil phallic emblems of oppression, their barrels fit for the insertion of flowers during times of protest.

I continued to venture outdoors with Roecker and Johnny Merwin and Jack Foster, but I learned quickly not to talk to others about it. The good old party was over. Not in rural America, not in the Texas of President Lyndon Johnson, the Wyoming of Dick Cheney, the Arkansas of future Governor Huckabee, or the Alaska of Sarah Palin. But in the cities and college towns all over America, the common assumption of the essential goodness of boys and men hunting together came under serious revision.

*Ah, well,* I used to think. *Where I come from, hunting is eternally normal.* And so I returned to Alberta expecting to revert to my old ways and escape the moral strictures of this strange new age. I also expected to return to hunting as soon as October arrived. But by this time, all of my regular nimrod buddies were either married and less available or off to live in other cities or both.

I got a job as a schoolteacher to pay off my student debts but foundered in the turbulent seas of hippydom, a stranger to his own world, with one foot in that good old time, when guys hunted with their buddies, and one foot in the bewilderingly hip present, where my old friends were sharing joints at parties as though nothing new had happened in my absence.

In the fall of 1969, I fell into an extended funk that lasted seven months. These bouts with melancholia are the writer's equivalent of an undergraduate degree. If nothing else, a good long depression serves to excise the perkiness from a young writer's prose. I'm not entirely comfortable with happiness, the emotion most frequently dramatized on television ads, but melancholia is okay with me, perhaps merely the downside of joy.

But in the fall of 1969, when I began my PhD, melancholia wasn't quite so innocuous. I would be struck dumb at gatherings and sleepwalk into the corners of rooms, and friends had to call me back from a long way off just to get a few words out of me. Every day at noon, I would wander into the student cafeteria and drink down a strawberry milkshake, and that was pretty much my sustenance for the day. I lost a lot of weight that year. Every once in a while, I managed to pull myself out of it and get a glimpse of what life could be like on the other side of the river.

Stoicism, like stubbornness, runs deep in the Carpenters. I should have been on Valium or something. I should have been seeing a counselor. I should have had the courage and good sense to know that when I was this bummed out, I needed to ask for help. But it fell on a handful of friends to keep me plugging along, and Al Purkess was among the best of these. Honest Al, we called him. He might have wondered if I was certifiable, but he never said so. I had met Honest Al in grade three, and there was scarcely ever a time that we weren't friends.

We both hated graduate school and liked the out-of-doors, so during that dismal time, Al managed to convince me to come out now and then and do a little weekend hunting. That year we had some early snow in October, and the ruffed grouse were at the peak of their cycle. After every snowfall there would be a melt, and the grouse would venture out of the bush to peck at the gravel and what was left of the clover that grew, still green, at the side of the trails and side roads. In those days I drove a beige Volkswagen Beetle, and it took a lot of abuse in the cause of hunting for sanity.

"Carp, see those trees on the left? Why don't you drop me off up there and drive back here, and I'll walk back toward you. Probably meet you at that old barn, eh?"

"Huh?"

"The barn. That old thing up there."

"Oh, right, the barn."

"Drive me up there, see? We can walk toward each other."

"Oh. Right."

In your urban existence you might well be a disenchanted grad student clad in regulation U.S. Army parka and sporting a scruffy beard. You might be overwhelmed by your own insignificance and harboring a mighty despair over the war in Vietnam, the state of your love life, the loss of some of your buddies to marriage, or the fallen world in general. You might have lost any reason whatsoever for getting out of bed in the morning, and you feel utterly alone in a world that feels less real with every day. You project this despair upon the entire world. But when you're carrying a loaded shotgun, there are many reasons for this gun not to go off and only one reason to fire it. For these few hours, you cannot afford the luxury of solipsism.

Al would be up there crashing through that grove of willows. He needs you to head upwind and stay alert for that first bird to flush. You have to know where he is. You have to stop and listen for the sound of large birds pattering through the leaves. You have to scan the tracks ahead of you in the melting snow. A magpie's tracks are long and thin, but a grouse's tracks are shaped like stars. You have to peer into the underbrush for anything that looks out of place, any movement, the smallest anomaly. You have to watch where you step and keep your index finger on the safety. As you get caught up in these hunters' imperatives, graduate student *Weltschmerz* drifts away like the smoke from your last joint. Somehow, for a few hours, life can be a simple proposition. Hunting with Al did not feel like therapy, but it was strangely therapeutic every time out.

With the help of a few friends like Honest Al, I stumbled out of the Stupid Zone and back into the grind. A few months later I was still a graduate student, still studying for my comprehensive exams, still hitting the books for my French qualifying exam, my German exam, still writing term papers that only a few people would ever read, still searching for a dissertation topic. But I was no longer certifiable.

I began looking around at other graduate students to detect signs of the same malaise from which I was just recovering. One fellow sufferer was Lennie Hollander, a dyed-in-the-wool bohemian from southern California. Since his arrival in Canada and his escape from the draft, Lennie had been a free spirit, a guitar picker, poet, and potter. But as the grind of grad school began to wear him down, he seemed to morph into an angry revolutionary. He saw conspiracies all over the place. His draft board in California was out to get him, the CIA was out to get him, his PhD advisory committee was out to get him, the campus cops, his landlord.

For many bright and bookish students back in the late sixties, graduate school was a kind of limbo. You didn't have a real job. If you were lucky, you could teach a first-year class for a pittance. You read stacks of books and enough interpretations of these books to fill a recycling bin, and then you wrote papers and exams that testified to your growing erudition. Many of us came to graduate school at this time seeking a community of scholars, perhaps a literary salon where we could debate the virtues of Proust until the bars closed.

Hunting?

Who among us would even admit that he had ever held a gun or shot at a deer? One gloomy night at the bar, under the influence of some weed Lennie had acquired, I admitted to him that I was a hunter. I tried to cast this confession in terms that Lennie might appreciate. I told him that up here, in the bush, you needed a gun for your own safety. A gross exaggeration, but in Lennie's presence I felt a need to justify my hunting habit. I told him about my encounter with the cougar in Jasper and threw in a few bear stories for good measure.

"I could get into that," said Lennie.

He was an admirer of Sam Shepard, the American playwright and actor who was living in Eastern Canada at the time and who had publicly extolled the virtues of hunting in the Maritimes. Our admiration for Sam Shepard was almost the only thing we had in common, except for our loathing of graduate school.

I had a hunch that a bit of hunting would be what the doctor ordered for my paranoid friend.

"Could you get me a gat?" he said.

A gat. Yes, I said, I could get him a gat. I managed to borrow an old twelve-gauge pump, and by Saturday morning we were headed north to find some ducks. I wore my brown canvas pants, matching hat, and canvas jacket with the red lining, the one that always seemed to have wheat chaff in the pockets. Lennie wore an army greatcoat that came down to his ankles and a Nazi helmet. He looked pretty bizarre for a guy on a hunting trip, especially a Jewish guy. But according to his wife, Martie, this coat was Lennie's only warm outerwear. And the helmet, Lennie claimed, would be good camouflage. But he was eager to cast his (clearly aberrant) decision to go hunting in some kind of acceptable political context. A campy parody of suburban manhood? A parody of militarism? A way of connecting him to the long-coated and misunderstood outlaws of the Old West?

Lennie had his doubts. When we drove into a grove of trees, brought out the binocs, and glassed our first slough, he must have realized that he was a long way from Los Angeles. When we clambered out of my Beetle and loaded our guns, he must have wondered if he was just having a bad dream or perhaps an acid flash. When a pair of mallards swung past us, however, he raised his gun well before I could get mine to my shoulder and fired, and down came his very first duck.

Lennie began to roar with laughter. I had heard him laugh sardonically before. I had heard him laugh in what seemed to me an imitation of a movie villain's cackle. I had heard Lennie laugh ironically, derisively, maniacally, and joylessly. But until the duck fell at our feet, I don't think that I had ever heard Lennie laugh joyfully. It was the laugh of a kid running through a sprinkler on a hot afternoon.

Lennie Hollander, my friend the fierce revolutionary, had become hooked on hunting. He was never entirely reconciled to it, never entirely comfortable with his role as slayer of ducks and pheasants. Still, when the grad student blues brought out Lennie's demons each autumn, he and I would head for the countryside with our guns and vent our despair, side by side, two neurotics on a country stroll. He never managed to bring capitalism to its knees, but he did keep a few demons at bay.

Lennie was not always available for hunting trips, and Honest Al had gone back into the world to become a teacher. So on the day I delivered my oral defense of my thesis topic, I was without a hunting buddy. Mort Ross, my thesis supervisor, urged me to take a few days off from grad studies and have some fun. I received this kindly advice in an old building known as Assiniboia Hall, just outside the main office of the English department. I'd had a haircut, I was clean shaven, and I was wearing a tie and tweed jacket and polished shoes with leather soles. That's what we looked like in those days when facing a roomful of scholars we needed to impress.

*Take off for a few days and have some fun.*

It was early November, pheasant season. There is an old hotel near the Badlands in Patricia, Alberta. It has a bar and a nice little restaurant. The proprietor in those days was Frenchie LaRue, a fine host and raconteur, and he barbecued the best steaks in the valley. His bar had a rancher motif, and all the ranchers in the area had burnt their brand into Frenchie's walls and tables. This cozy little hotel is just a short drive from the Red Deer River valley and Dinosaur Park, and it was home to some of the best pheasant hunting in Canada.

All I had time for was to throw my hunting equipment into my Beetle. If I hurried down there, I could arrive before dark. So I drove all the way to Patricia dressed in my academic finery. What would I look like to the men in Frenchie's bar? A member of the English gentry? A Bible salesman? I drove as fast as I could, and by the time I had driven all the way down to Highway 36 and hit the gravel road to Patricia, the sun was still hovering over the southwest horizon, giving the leafless hawthorn bushes a tangerine glow. I slowed down and began to enjoy the scenery, the sagebrush, cottonwoods, and cactus in the coulees. My frenzy of unpreparedness had dissipated, and I knew that I would be sipping a beer in Frenchie's hotel within the hour. I was at last relaxed.

And then a cock pheasant trotted across the gravel road in front of me.

When you load up a shotgun and you're wearing a shirt, tie, and jacket, you can't avoid looking like a cop, and perhaps also a real crazy. I walked over to the ditch at the side of the road. There was a nice accommodating skim of snow on the ground. I spotted the big three-pronged tracks of my rooster. He was heading for some cattails up the road. If I could head him off before he reached the heavy cover of the cattails, I had a chance of putting him up. I began to hoof it. Just before I arrived at the cattails, he flew up in front of me. I slid to a stop, clicked off the safety, aimed, and fired. My pheasant hit the ground, winged and running. Damn.

Scrambling and sliding in my polished shoes, I gave chase along the road. The rooster disappeared into the cattails, but his blood trail came out the other side and continued as far as a culvert. Instead of running down the culvert under the road, however, my wounded pheasant tried to hide under a brush pile. Some flecks of blood in the snow betrayed this last turn he had taken. Spotting the last few inches of his long tail, I leapt into the pile of brush, grabbed him by the legs, and hauled him out. I wrung his neck and bagged him, my first pheasant of the year.

Just as I was placing my empty gun back into the car, I caught a glimpse of myself in the side mirror. My shirt and tie were flecked with blood, and my slacks were newly studded with brambles and seeds and God only knows what kind of fluff. Pheasant hackles were clinging to my nice tweed jacket. Lennie Hollander would have been amused. Bill Roecker and Johnny Merwin would have laughed themselves into exhaustion. And my dad would surely have wondered where he and Mum had gone wrong.

What sort of a grotesque had I become? As the days passed down in Patricia, I hunted alone and supped with other hunters who had come down there with their buddies. I envied them their camaraderie. I realized that I needed a new hunting buddy.

IF THE TERM *extreme hunting* had been current in the late sixties and early seventies, its greatest practitioner would have been Mosey Walcott from somewhere up in northern Michigan. Like Lennie Hollander and me, he was a real malcontent as a graduate student. Perhaps the burden of so many exams in so many languages, with such a wide array of literature to master, was beginning to try him. I know it got to me, and if the burden of graduate studies brought out the neurotic in me, it brought out a persona in Mo that was half bear and half Boon Hogganbeck. He was crazy for hunting and fishing and a real jock to boot, a competitive swimmer, built like a wrestler. And oddly enough, a literary scholar. But it was his ursine ways that I found most fascinating.

During a prolonged stretch of grad student malaise and domestic unease, Mo accompanied his wife to a company picnic in the country. It took place at a campground surrounded by spruce trees near the North Saskatchewan River somewhere southwest of Edmonton. Dozens of Mo's wife's colleagues and their families had descended upon this lovely spot, and they were all roasting wieners and having a merry time.

In his depressed state, Mo should never have gone. His wife should have left him at home with the kids. But he went, and they all roasted wieners and marshmallows and drank beer, and at a certain moment in the evening as the darkness descended on the happy campers, Mo rose up, grabbed a very large jug of wine, and lumbered into the woods to drink and ponder.

I like to imagine this scene happening beneath a full and raging moon. Mo was lurching through the trees, stopping to gulp his wine, and reflecting upon life, when he became possessed by a new identity. Perhaps a frontier version of Mr. Hyde. He heard some grunting in the bush and a prolonged, high-pitched growl, so he crawled into a thicket and drank and listened some more. At last he realized that the grunting and growling were coming from his own throat.

Indeed, he had become a bear. And not just any bear but the very essence and spirit of bear, universally known and feared throughout the world. Armed with this knowledge—*I am Bear*—he arose from the thicket, hurled his empty jug into the moonlight, and lumbered back toward the campground, where, from the top of someone's station wagon, he beheld the great tribe of hairless ones with whom he had so recently been picnicking.

He needed to proclaim himself to this tribe as a newly born bear. He needed them to know that he was no longer of their blood and their ways. I like to imagine him as divesting himself of all but his running shoes, a youthful Lear on the heath, filled with mischief and confusion and predatory power. Well, anyway, filled with an awful lot of cheap wine.

He noticed that some women were giggling at him. "Oh, he's just a teddy bear!" one of them tittered. He rushed them on all fours and they fled, screaming, back to the party. Galloping behind them among the parked cars, still on all fours, Mo emerged into the light of the campfire. He leapt onto a picnic table surrounded by joyous members of his former species and roared at the top of his lungs.

His memory of this scene is not sharp. But one detail of his oft-repeated account always caught my attention. The people gathered around the picnic table were so unnerved by his presence that they kept on talking, pretending that what they saw was not really there. Or if there, it was just this big man's little joke. Ha ha ha. But the nervous laughter died down, and they backed away from the table, and that was the end of the evening for all of them.

After this episode, Mo's wife suggested he find a hobby. So Mo bought a shotgun.

In the fall of 1971, he too needed a hunting buddy, and as a fellow malcontent in the same department and with an office near his, I was the natural choice. We had been working out a bit together, so we were beginning to get to know each other. Working out with weights and running was all new to me, but Mo seemed to know everything there was to know about fitness.

I never hunted with Mo Walcott, Lennie Hollander, and Honest Al all together—never even introduced them to one another. My friendships with all three were kept discrete and compartmentalized. There's nothing much wrong with potassium nitrate or sulfur or charcoal, but I wouldn't mix them together unless I wanted a big blowup. I guess what I'm talking about here is political dissonance.

Anyway, Mo Walcott was my last sporting life buddy before I left Alberta in 1973. He and I hunted and fished many times together before the Fates took us in opposite directions, and I lost track of him. We had great success on these trips, and our last hunt was almost the only one in which the quarry eluded us.

We had thrown up a tent in the ranching country west of Rocky Mountain House and east of the Rockies, good terrain back then for ambushing mallards and putting up ruffed grouse. But during our first night in the tent, a weather system moved in and we woke up on the day of our hunt to below-zero temperatures and a skim of new snow. This weather system had sent all the mallards south for the winter.

Our only option was to drive to the Upper Stoney Creek valley and walk the cut lines. Back then this area was good moose-hunting territory. If one looked hard enough, a fair number of black bears and even the occasional grizzly could be found ambling through these woods. If I remember correctly, several hours of walking produced only one grouse, which for Mo and me was unusual. We had lunch in the bush and continued to walk the cut lines, but by about four thirty the sun was sinking, and so were our prospects. I was aching to get back to the car, and I told this to Mo.

"C'mon, Carp," he said, "don't jam out on me."

There is an impulse among the keenest of hunters when they are young—an impulse that Roderick Haig-Brown came to deplore. It is the urge simply to kill something and to do it even if they have to hunt from dusk on to midnight. I knew that urge, and perhaps I was trying to leave it behind. But the urge was upon my buddy Mo. He ambled farther into the bush, and so, reluctantly, I followed. There was not enough snow

114 · A HUNTER'S CONFESSION

among the trees to spot the silhouettes of grouse, and as the light faded into a gray dusk that matched the heavy clouds above us and the heavy shadows in the woods and the mist rising from the nearby creek, Mo became more and more determined.

"Carp," he said to me, "you go that way and turn left up by that marshy shit and then walk back toward me. Okay?"

I was bone weary and still aching for the warmth of the car, but arguing with Mo was futile. How do you stop a force of nature from doing what comes naturally?

I didn't grasp the answer to this question until I reached the marsh and spotted some animal tracks in the snow. The tracks got me thinking. They were everywhere, and they were surprisingly visible in the faded light. Deer tracks, moose tracks, rabbit tracks, and some small delicate pawprints that might have been made by a fox. Thank God there were no bear tracks.

Bear tracks. Hmm.

Maybe I had something there. I got down on my knees, pulled out my jackknife, tore off my gloves, and began to muck around with the heels of my hands until I had my creation pretty much on the money: a set of fake grizzly tracks that seemed to dissolve at the edge of the marsh. Front paws abbreviated like the feet of a giant walking on tiptoes, back paws massive rounded triangles with five toes. My knife was just the right tool to create the clawmarks. They were quite inspired, if I do say so myself. To get a bear to back down, you see, you need an even bigger bear.

"Mo!" I hollered. "You better see this!"

He came tromping through the bush, his gun at the ready.

"Whatcha got there, Carp?"

I pointed to the tracks.

Mo released a long string of words so profane they were almost lyrical.

Warily, I looked his way, because I thought he was onto my con and swearing at me. But instead of anger and suspicion on his face, there was fascination, there was awe—as though he had seen the lair of the dark gods. He got down on his knees and stared.

Then he got up.

"Carp, this bastard must weigh a friggin ton!"

He said that more than once.

"Carp, I think we had better get the hell outta here."

I bowed to his wisdom, and we retraced our footsteps all the way back to the car.

And that was that. My last act as a hunter before I left Alberta forever was to counterfeit the tracks of a grizzly. Johnny Merwin would have enjoyed the joke. He would have been proud of me.

I don't miss the sixties: the graduate student melancholia, the futility, the politics, the craziness of that time. But I do miss the way I coped with that time, which amounted to tromping through the fields and woods with a gun and a buddy. Honest Al and I live in different cities. We stay in touch, but we don't hunt together anymore. I don't know where Mo and Lennie have gone. After I left Oregon and returned to Canada, I learned that Johnny Merwin's wife had shot and killed him in a domestic dispute. He's been dead for almost forty years. I heard a rumor in the 1980s that Bill Roecker had moved to California. Once, at a fishing resort, I saw his name on the register and the following notation: *Had a great time. I lost Larry Lunker just north of the beaver house. See you again.*

I am talking about hunting during a specific time in North America when assumptions about life were changing irrevocably. And since the late 1960s these changes have solidified into something like an orthodoxy. As the American writer Matthew Teague says in his essay "A More Dangerous Game," attitudes "have shifted and hardened, and the very idea of hunting as 'sport' has come to imply something cavalier. Among animal rights advocates it indicated indifference to wildlife. In two generations the lone hunter—once exemplified by Teddy Roosevelt—found himself accused of enmity toward nature. Hunting [has] become a question of morality."

These American friends of mine in the late 1960s and early 1970s have lumbered off into the mists. But for a brief and difficult time in our lives, we were throwbacks together, and for the sanity that craziness brought me I will always be grateful. We all thought that hunting was strictly a guy thing, and in this belief we were (I blush to admit) singleminded. But our little orthodoxy was about to be reformed.

# 6 THE RETURN OF ARTEMIS

*To squeeze the trigger or not, to embrace that bittersweet
burden of mutual mortality and make a meal of it, or to let it be.
These are decisions not lightly, or easily, undertaken—
especially, perhaps, when the gun is in a woman's hands.*

MARY ZEISS STANGE, *Woman the Hunter*

ON A road trip with my wife, Honor, in the fall of 1997,
we came upon a big flight of Canada geese in a field.
We had a shotgun in the car and some goose shells for just this
eventuality, because Honor had decided to try her hand at
hunting.

We are talking here about an urban feminist who
loves critters. Given a wide array of hunting stories, she
would cheer for the animals every time. But something
had changed.

After years of Honor's resisting the hunt, her curiosity must have gotten the better of her. A year or two
earlier, she decided to come along with Bill Robertson and me and observe a grouse shoot at close hand,
and this excursion seemed to open a door for her. In

the months that followed, she took her firearms safety course and passed the written exam and the target practice sessions with flying colors, and now she had her first hunting license.

But back to the fall of 1997. The geese were feeding on a large spread with very little cover, a couple of hundred greater Canadas scattered over the middle of the field. The farmer who had given us permission told Honor that her best chance lay in crawling along a windbreak until she was within shooting range. She was okay with all of this, and I watched her head for the windbreak and then go down on elbows and knees. I felt at the time that I should not accompany her, that she should make all the decisions on her own. I remained in the car and pulled out my binoculars. Like the stealthiest of night raiders, she elbowed and crabbed forward on her belly all the way to the end of the windbreak in knee-high grass. I was a bit surprised, I suppose, at how eagerly she took on this mission and even more surprised that I was content to sit and watch.

She disappeared into the grass and then suddenly reappeared, hauled herself up to a standing position, and threw the gun to her shoulder. The clamor of barking geese and the gun's reports came to me in a split-second delay, but suddenly the booming sky was full of birds and pellets. She got off three shots, reloaded, and fired again, but no damage was done. She stood there in the silence staring at the receding wave of geese. I think the farmer was pleased.

As I watched Honor return to the car, I expected to see some evidence of dejection.

Her first words were, "That was amazing!"

Her cheeks were flushed bright red, and her eyes were blazing with excitement. Her frustration at not killing a goose was merely a small part of the mix. *Frenzy*, I thought to myself. The same wild frenzy I felt when I went out to shoot with the men—this was the first time I had seen it on the face of a hunting woman. In the separate places she and I grew up, girls were not encouraged to hunt with their dads or anyone else.

Honor's father, Bill Kever, used to be a keen hunter in Idaho. He married a woman from an English village in the Midlands whom he had met when he was stationed there during the war. Her name was Honor Martin. She and Bill settled in Boise, Idaho, in the late 1940s and lived there during a time when the mallard and pheasant hunting was very good.

One weekend, Bill decided to take his wife hunting with a couple of friends and their wives. I will never know who first suggested this plan and how much Bill hesitated before taking Honor out with him. She had never shot before, so he decided that she might be most usefully deployed putting up pheasants.

The first sign that this outing might not unfold as she had imagined was what she referred to as the *Hunter's Bloody Rule of Silence*. What was the point of going out for a hunt with your husband and his friends if you couldn't *talk* with them? Honor senior *loved* to talk. Things went downhill from there when she entered the bush, heard the boom of shotguns nearby, and realized that her job was to be their hunting dog. She never returned to the field.

I followed a different plan with her daughter, Honor junior. I bought her a sixteen-gauge pump gun, and as soon as she learned to shoot skeet, she took to hunting with real enthusiasm. Perhaps she managed to connect with her dad's love for the hunt as I had done with my dad. But how many years she must have taken to uncover that desire to hunt birds with a shotgun. How she must have fought against all those decades of socializing when girls were told what they should and should not do.

Honor went from goose hunting to hunting with a rifle for whitetails and really got into the excitement of it for several years before her eyes betrayed her. She could read fine with glasses, and she could see into the distance with or without binoculars, but she discovered that she could no longer sight down a barrel, fix her eyes to the bead at the end of the barrel, and train the gun on the bird or animal she was hunting all at the same time. Her eyes had turned middle-aged on her, and she moved on to other pastimes without regret. Honor never thought of herself as a dyed-in-the-wool hunter, but some of her favorite stories of all time have come from her brief participation in the hunt. Back in my bachelor days, a couple of my girlfriends had hunted with me, but only as noncombatants. Like Honor—like most contemporary women—they had never been encouraged by their fathers or their brothers to learn how to shoot.

Reading about sport hunting in North America in the 1940s, '50s, and '60s, we don't often see women mentioned. They were supposed to be the ones the hunter returned to in defeat or triumph. This kind of hunting had been largely about male bonding, or the male quest, or fun and adventure for men of leisure. In England, upper-class women of the last century frequently went shooting with the men and just as frequently rode on the fox hunts. But in North America, most female hunters have been Aboriginal. My former office-mate, Maria Campbell, the Métis writer, used to tell me about the women in her family who shot a moose each year to help their families get through the winter.

In most early-twentieth-century accounts of Aboriginal hunting practices up north among Cree and Dene people, the men would leave the encampment to range as far from their tents as they needed to go to kill the largest animals (moose, bear, caribou, and beaver). The women, in most of these communities, would remain with the children and prepare their meals, mend clothing and tents, and gather berries and other food necessary for their family's diet. But many of the women had guns, and they hunted to feed their families. Often this meant taking a shotgun out into the bush near the camp and shooting grouse or ptarmigan or taking a rifle after porcupine or deer. Their hunting and gathering was in no way subordinate to that of the men, who went farther afield in search of bigger game.

In many hunter-gatherer cultures, from Australia and the Bay of Bengal to the Upper Amazon and Labrador, children would learn their early skills from their mothers, but at a certain age, the boys would go off with their fathers and the hunting men of their tribe to learn hunting skills. This arrangement allowed both parents to share the burden of child care. Thus began the division of labor between female gatherers and male hunters in an Aboriginal settlement.

In some tribal cultures—in Botswana and Namibia, for example—there were taboos against women touching men's weapons used for hunting, but other native cultures had no such taboos. Batek women in Malaysia used blowpipes for hunting, just like the men, but they seemed to prefer digging out squirrels, bamboo rats, porcupine, and turtles and whacking them with their digging tools. Inuit women learned to hunt, or not, according to the needs of their families. A man with daughters and no sons would train his girls to hunt with him. In the desert regions of Western Australia, men hunted with spears and women hunted with dogs. The dogs would run down the prey, and the women would dispatch the animals with clubs. The Agta women of the Philippines were full participants with the men in the hunt and used the same hunting dogs, bows, arrows, and machetes as the men did. But like the mythical Amazon warriors, these women were the exception rather than the rule. Tribal societies granting women equal status as hunters were unusual, but tribal societies in which women participated in the hunt, at some level, were many.

Too often social scientists tell us that men were the hunters and women were the gatherers. Anthropologists, paleo-anthropologists, eco-feminists, ethnologists, and all kinds of other academics have advanced this model for a variety of contending reasons. So when we read accounts of women hunting in hunter-gatherer societies, we might be tempted to think that these women are an aberration or a huge exception to the rule.

Anthropologists will sometimes tell us that men hunt meat but women gather it—even if the meat in question is the same species. This suggestion conjures up a picture of doughty men spearing kangaroos and women shopping for kangaroo burger at the nearest mall. Cultural forces, tribal and intellectual, have been at play for a long time to exclude women from the hunt.

In North American hunting cultures, among Aboriginals, this exclusion might have begun when the rifle arrived in great numbers on the plains. The writer and cultural analyst Deborah Homsher reminds us that "there are very few tales of nineteenth-century Native American women shooting guns. Those times when they did ride with the war parties, they were more likely to be involved holding or stealing horses." Gun technology, Homsher observes, worked to "alienate Plains men from women, for it empowered the galloping, shooting men who showed youth, daring, and self-concern, thus decreasing cooperation and encouraging a kind of individualism inside the tribal circle."

LET'S PUT IT this way: if we have come to believe that hunting, like soldiering, is for the most part a gender-specific activity, we can always find exceptions to this rule, and these exceptions keep emerging among women of every conceivable class, color, and persuasion. We see this happening in spite of what we are told to expect.

Here is one example. All over North America the number of recreational hunters is dropping. The decline has been dramatic. It began four or five decades ago and continues to this day. But one of the exceptions to this trend is the number of women who have begun to take up hunting. Since the early 1990s, according to Mary Zeiss Stange's survey, the number of women who hunt has gone from about 3 percent to 12 percent of the total hunting population.

This figure has been called into question (by Homsher), because the exact number is very hard to run down. It appears probable, however, that at least fifteen million American women now own guns. And during a time when men are increasingly hanging up their guns, several million women are now hunting.

Mary Zeiss Stange speaks about her own choice to become a hunter. It's a story that a number of modern urban women can identify with. She was a city girl from New Jersey with no knowledge of guns or hunting, and then, at age thirty-three, she married a man who loved to hunt, who had a five thousand-acre ranch in Montana. Stange's conversion to the gun was gradual.

> I liked getting exercise, enjoyed the outdoors and loved the birds and venison [her husband, Doug] brought home. One thing led to another, and before I knew it, there I was, busting through in grouse country behind our springer spaniel, crouching in frosty reeds watching the sun rise on the opening day of waterfowl season and crawling on my belly through prickly pear cactus to get within 200 yards of a herd of pronghorns. Now, after 15 years afield, hunting is a passion I cannot imagine I ever did without.

Mary Zeiss Stange is a professor of Women's Studies and Religion at Skidmore College and a strong feminist. She is not comfortable with how women have been designated by various social scientists who seem eager to take women out of the hunting picture altogether. According to the hunting hypothesis described in Chapter 2, prehistoric women were biologically fated to be gatherers and men biologically determined to be hunters. This vision of Paleolithic bliss was consistent with how these social scientists saw their wives in modern times: the woman as helpmate. Teddy Roosevelt put it this way:

> The man must be glad to do a man's work, to dare and endure and to labor; to keep himself, and to keep those dependent upon him. The woman must be the housewife, the helpmate of the home-maker, the wise and fearless mother of many children . . . When men fear to work or fear righteous war, when women fear motherhood, they tremble on the brink of doom; and well it is that they should vanish from the earth.

Anyone who argues that males should be defined by their aggressiveness and females by their passivity will find themselves fixed in Mary Stange's crosshairs. "Macho males," she says, "perceive the advantage of keeping women out of the field. Perish the thought that women might take up arms, become skilled in their use, and become . . . able to defend themselves *and* to fend for themselves! Woman the Hunter . . . is a profoundly unsettling figure, her wildness a force to be reckoned with."

Apparently she is unsettling to women as well, especially radical feminists, eco-feminists, and animal rights advocates who believe that women's hunting—indeed, any hunting—is a moral outrage. These thinkers argue that there are essential differences between women and men. Woman the gatherer is the womb of true humanity, and the bond between her and her child is the foundation of human society. This model is set in opposition to male hunters' savagery and men's violence in general. Essentially, men hunt down wild animals and kill them. Essentially, women gather wild edible plants and nurture children. This essentialist model starts to look like the stuff of Teddy Roosevelt's dreams. Any acceptance of "the essential differences between women and men is grounded, however unwittingly," says Stange, "in precisely those categories feminism seeks to overturn."

It's time for a new woman to emerge. It's time for Artemis to return from her long exile. She is the moon goddess, the virgin goddess, the fleet-footed goddess of the hunt. Some call her the huntress, but I'm trying my best to avoid that term; it's like referring to Sharon Olds or Margaret Atwood as a poetess.

Remember the paradox that hunters kill that which they love? Well, Artemis is the embodiment of that riddle. She is both the stalker who slays the wild animals with bow and arrow and the protector of those animals. Artemis's virginity is emblematic of the places she protects—the wild virgin forests, their mountains and rivers. When Orion bragged that he would kill every wild animal he could find, Artemis overheard him and took him down. When Actaeon, also a hunter, surprised Artemis bathing in her stream, she turned him into a stag, and his own dogs took him down.

She is also known as the women's goddess, associated as she is with the phases of the moon, the rites of menstruation, childbirth, and nurturing. When she is not at work protecting the wild animals, she protects childbearing women. Mess with animals or women, you have Artemis to deal with.

Don't mess with Ms. Stange either. She has elbowed her way into the space between disapproving patriarchs and disapproving feminists. She is a gun advocate, a hunting advocate, and a feminist who gathers and hunts with equal abandon.

TO RESEARCH HER book *Women & Guns: Politics and the Culture of Firearms in America,* Deborah Homsher has immersed herself in the class issues, the history, and the polemics of women and guns. Unlike Stange, who is a fervent advocate, Homsher is a writer whose objectivity on the subject of women who hunt is her strongest suit. She finds as many examples of women banding together to restrict the availability of guns as women who are gun-ho, like Stange and Carol Oyster. What Stange voices on behalf of the army of elite professional women who now go hunting, Homsher reports on behalf of a much wider array of females, including ordinary working-class women, small-town women, and farm women. They hunt near home. Their reasons for hunting are as variable as their lives. They hunt to fill the pot.

They hunt to protect their livestock from varmints. They hunt to be a part of the annual rituals that their fathers and brothers have always enjoyed. They hunt to be with their husbands. Their hunting is part of what makes them real as rural women, part of their authenticity. Many of them live in households where guns are kept without any stigma, which is probably more common than in middle-class urban households. These women seem to live outside the debates about gun regulation, gun registration, gun ownership, anti- and pro-gun politics.

In one interview with four female hunters, Homsher questioned them about who might have influenced them to buy guns and use guns for hunting. "I mentioned to Stefani, Joan, Carol, and Shirley that many people considered the gun organizations' interest in women to be part of an ugly marketing ploy, a trick to convince women that guns could actually protect them from harm, when . . . studies showed that household guns increased chances for tragedy." The interviewees insisted that women were not being urged by men to take up guns but were actively seeking information about them. It was anti-gun liberals who assumed that these women were being duped by men.

One of Homsher's hunter-interviewees, Shirley Grenoble, began hunting in the 1950s, when women were seen infrequently in the field. Men would ask her why she would go out "shooting a man's deer." Her reply to Homsher was that "it was what I wanted to do because I *liked* it."

Most of the women Homsher interviewed in her study were enthusiastic about shooting, but as I mentioned earlier, they tended to live outside the gun debates, the pro- and anti-gun politics that have garnered so much attention in the news media. Sometimes male hunters with conservative views of women disapproved of them, sometimes anti-gun liberals disapproved of them, but not many outsiders could get a real handle on them.

Homsher's interviews in *Women & Guns* and Mary Zeiss Stange's stories in *Woman the Hunter* make me wonder if the growing contingent of female hunters on this continent isn't perhaps a register of women's resurgence as a political force in a time when there is a more relaxed atttitude to what women do with their lives. The Artemis factor can move in and bedevil our notions about the quintessential masculine and feminine.

A man needs to be careful making assumptions about women. A man who is a writer needs to be twice as careful. As I wrote this chapter, in a moment of uncertainty, I decided to test what I had read about women who hunt—especially what I had read in Stange's and Homsher's work.

From Stange's two books (including the one she wrote with Carol Oyster), I came to envision an enthusiastic army of women, several million of them, taking up the gun. Stange gives us the narrative of the embattled woman determined to hunt animals amid a chorus of highly politicized unbelievers, disapproving patriarchs on the one side and radical feminists on the other. She and many women of equal determination emerge victorious, but not without dodging some slings and arrows from their detractors. The woman who chooses hunting becomes stigmatized, vilified, or ignored—the pariah of women's and gender studies departments, the scourge of the PETA-philes. But the Artemisian sisterhood prevails in the end.

Homsher tries to maintain some emotional distance from the politics of women and guns in order to examine these politics. She lets her women tell their stories. Some people disapprove of the women who hunt and their nimrod ways, but this disapproval doesn't deter the women from hunting. Homsher's women don't seem to be much aware of the organizations that Stange talks about—the National Rifle Association, the BOW program (Becoming an Outdoors-Woman), or the many local organizations that teach women all about guns and hunting.

But I was mentioning my moment of uncertainty, the kind of uncertainty a fellow might sense when attempting to say something conclusive about women. In such moments we fellows band together and bolster each other's wisdom, or, in the absence of wisdom, we just plain bolster.

Through my friend Jake MacDonald (fiction writer, memoirist, outdoor writer, hunter) I met Ruthanne and Barbara Hanbidge, a mother and daughter who have hunted for many years in Saskatchewan. Ruthanne is now in her eighties, and her daughter is in the healthy prime of middle age. Both women are radiant with good health and have the well-tanned faces of people who spend a lot of time outside. Strong women. Their features seem to be shaped and toned by the prairie wind.

Ruthanne began hunting with her dad in rural Saskatchewan when she was a girl. Her father taught her all she needed to know about gun safety when she was in her early teens. When she was seventeen, he bought her a twenty-gauge shotgun, which marked the beginning of a preoccupation she would pursue for the next seventy years.

I say *preoccupation* because I'm at a loss for words here. *Sport? Hobby? Recreation?* These words seem too limp for a pursuit so captivating that it amounts to a way of life for these women. *Passion* is a better word. They are somewhat akin to the women Deborah Homsher spoke with: they are not out to make a statement or embattled from too much moral disapproval. They hunt because they want to.

Ruthanne hunted regularly with her father and two brothers. Her older sisters were not nearly as keen to go hunting with their father. "You know," she says, "Oh, eek, blood and stuff." Ruthanne admits that it was unusual for a girl or a woman to hunt in the 1940s and 1950s. But rarely did Ruthanne or her daughter Barbara ever feel stigmatized as hunting women. Nor do they believe there is much difference between hunting with men and hunting with women. Indeed, the only people who disapprove of their hunting ways are people who disapprove of all hunting.

Both women laugh about a neighbor who grew up next to the Hanbidge house in Saskatoon. The woman in question returned home for a wedding shower to which Ruthanne had been invited. "All I remember about your house when I was a girl," she said to Ruthanne, "was that every time I looked out the window, there was always something *dead* hanging in your backyard."

Ruthanne never brags about a successful hunt. She claims that "too many people will come up and say, 'Oh, how could you?'"

But hunting with men is okay with Ruthanne. "They're good at hauling."

"Seriously," says daughter Barbara, "hauling a deer up a ravine was fine twenty years ago, but now me and Mum aren't so spry." Mother and daughter are laughing, and Barbara continues, "I'd say, 'Why did you shoot that deer at the *bottom* of the coulee? What the *heck* did you do that for?'"

The only people these women have tried to avoid hunting with were incompetent hunters, men or women. Ruthanne tells the story of a mule-deer hunt in the Great Sand Hills of southwestern Saskatchewan. She and her husband, Robert, had walked a couple of miles into the hills and were sitting on some high ground. They heard the approach of all-terrain vehicles, and Robert said, "I'll bet they're going to chase some deer our way." Sure enough, some deer came by, and Ruthanne dropped one next to a woody little copse. They went down into the brush so that Ruthanne could tag her deer. "All of a sudden, bullets started to zoom and whiz at us. You see, these guys in the ATVs thought we were deer."

Ruthanne never hunted there again. She lost her enthusiasm for hunting antelope one day when one of her hunting companions fired willy-nilly into a herd of pronghorns. "He liked to shoot into a herd and they'd all run away, and one or two animals would be running on broken legs. Not for me, no thanks."

Barbara and Ruthanne recounted tales of people who overshot their limits, people who would rather chase animals from their vehicles than walk out into the field, or wealthy hunters so obsessed with the number of points on a rack that they'd only go for trophy mounts. "Like hunting was always some kind of competition," says Ruthanne. She and Barbara think that trophy hunting and mounting heads are a guy thing.

Whether Aboriginal or not, whether recreational hunters or subsistence hunters, very few North American women in my experience have voiced an interest in trophy hunting. It began in England with scientists, some of whom were sportsmen, gathering samples of birds and animals for scientific research in the nineteenth century. Many of these gentlemen were educated, enthusiastic amateurs with private incomes and a great deal of leisure time. English sportsmen brought this earnest pursuit to North America, where they collected trophy heads in the name of science, but the collecting became an end in itself, a kind of monomania in which far too many animals were sacrificed at the altar of the male ego.

Women tend more to hunt for meat. A great meal, a winter full of good meals, is the ultimate reward. "The best eating is a good-sized doe or a young buck," says Barbara. A big buck would taste fine, she added, "but only if you brought it down fast and clean. You don't want them to run injured." Barbara used to show a preference for fresh deer liver fried up with onions and juniper berries. (These days, with chronic wasting disease in evidence on the prairies, the livers need to be tested first.) Ruthanne loves sharptail breasts fried up on the Coleman.

Both women love to hunt for the experience. To Barbara this means simply being in the out-of-doors, learning new things about nature each time, feeling part of the ecosystem. Gail McConnell told me the same thing back in the 1980s about her own hunting expeditions in southern Saskatchewan. I took many years to reach that same conclusion: hunting is consistently fun regardless of whether blood is spilled. Eating, however, is more delightful if blood has been spilled.

I asked Barbara and Ruthanne if they ever experienced a moment of regret at pulling the trigger and killing a wild creature.

"Every time," says Barbara. "I don't like to kill *per se*; I respect the animals, but I'm hunting for food, and I'm not going to wait around for the deer to die of old age."

Hunting, to Barbara and Ruthanne, and most members of the Hanbidge extended family, is a great gift, not a right. They are among the fortunate few who live in a place where they can get up early and go hunting for geese or deer and be back and in time to go to work.

Ruthanne's children and her grandchildren have all been lovingly taught to respect and appreciate nature. One of her granddaughters tells of crawling out into the weeds and stubble one day just to see how close she could come to a flock of sandhill cranes. This bloodless stalking is something Ruthanne has done many times. Once, on point at a deer run, waiting for the right animal to show up, she spotted a big buck strolling her way.

She was downwind and she didn't move, so the buck came within a hundred feet before it wandered off.

"Why didn't you shoot it?" one of the men asked her.

"I just wanted to look," she said.

I have posed some of the above questions to my male hunting buddies. What kind of animals do you shoot at? Trophy heads or good meat? What kind of deer do you hope to bring down for a good meal? Are there moments of regret when you pull the trigger on a bird or an animal? Ian Pitfield, Peter Nash, Terry Myles, and Doug Elsasser all said roughly the same thing, with some variations. I really have to dig to come up with differences between how men hunt and how women hunt, what they prefer, what they avoid.

Most of the trophy hunters are men, and most of the hunters who are keen on mounting heads are men. Most of the hunters who are so competitive that they count points on a rack before squeezing the trigger are men. These competitive urges do not describe my own friends who hunt; they describe an old-school demographic of primarily wealthy hunters who continue to reenact the male quest experience as Roosevelt and Hemingway had done. They remind me that there are genuine differences between male and female attitudes to hunting, but I want to be careful not to make too much of these differences.

Ruthanne Hanbidge gave me her take on the increased number of women who take to hunting: "Now that women are out there in the workforce, they know they can do anything." If Artemis still haunts the virgin forests, she is probably smiling.

# 7 THE LAST GREAT HUNTER

*He had learned that they would head for the
Sweet Grass Hills. The grass was always long there, and the
buffalo caused the plains to be black as far as one could see.*
JAMES WELCH, *Fools Crow*, Part 1

*For three more sleeps I followed this strange Napikwan
[white man] that leaves his meat. He killed a long-tail, a bighead, three
real-dogs and five wags-his-tails. He even tried to kill your brother,
Skunk Bear, but I flew ahead and warned him. In anger, the Napikwan
took a shot at me, scared the shit out of me, so I left. But for
many moons now the hunter kills animals until they become
scarce . . . He will kill us all off if something isn't done.*
JAMES WELCH, *Fools Crow*, Part 2

*But there were no [buffalo]. And there were no longlegs
and no bighorns. There were no wags-his-tails or prairie-runners.
It was as if the earth had swallowed up the animals.*
JAMES WELCH, *Fools Crow*, Part 4

DURING THE 1970s, I taught English classes all over northern Manitoba and Saskatchewan. I would travel by plane or by bus. Most of the time I could do my preparations on the way up and grade papers on the way down.

In one of these communities up in the boreal forest, I used to eat lunch with my students in the cafeteria. It was part of an old convent that had been converted into a college residence. My students were all about my own age, mostly Métis or nonstatus Cree, and most of them boarded in the convent. One day in the late fall, the talk turned to a fellow named Jojo Mitewin, a hunter who apparently lived in a shack between the town and the reserve.

"He won't never shoot a bear," one woman told me.

I asked her why, and she recounted the following story.

When Jojo was young, he used to hunt with her uncle, who was now deceased. They had a big wooden transport canoe propelled by an old kicker. They would run the canoe up the river against the current for a whole day and paddle back slowly for a few days' hunting. This way they could descend through some good hunting habitat without the noise from the kicker, and when the hunting was done, they would be practically home again. They knew where the wetlands lay in relation to the river valley, and these places were best for moose. There were more moose than either elk or caribou up there, but more elk and caribou than deer, and all kinds of beaver as well.

On this particular trip, Jojo and the old man went farther upstream than usual. On the first day, paddling back downstream, they stopped, and one of them shot a beaver. He gutted it and jammed the carcass under a canoe seat. The canoe was beached at an old crossing, so the river ran shallow in this place. Jojo Mitewin (pronounced MEE-ta-ween) and the narrator's uncle hiked back up to the beaver dam to see if there was any moose sign. They found nothing and returned to the canoe. But a big male black bear was waiting for them. He had his two front paws in their canoe, and he was knocking things around to get at the beaver carcass. They yelled at the bear, but he just looked their way and returned to his task.

Jojo shot the bear. He said he had no choice. He kept saying that. The bear would have stoved in the canoe, and the two men would have had a very hard time getting back, and they were a long way from home. Jojo had shot the bear in the chest, but the bear still had something left in him. He stumbled out of the canoe and ran across to the other side of the river.

The men knew that they had to kill the bear, put it out of its misery. You don't leave an animal wounded in the woods, especially not a bear. They had to cross the river in the shallow water and go into the bush and find that bear and kill it—a dangerous thing to do. The bush was very thick, but they made out some drops of blood here and there. At last Jojo heard a sound of moaning. The two men closed in and saw the bear lying beneath a big fallen tree. It was moaning like a man. Those were Jojo's words. *It was moaning like a man.*

I forget the name of the woman who told the story. But I remember, roughly, these words: "Up here, ah? The old people? They don't like to kill a bear. They think the bear might be their uncle or their Kokom or their grandfather." The woman made it clear to me that she did not believe in this bullshit.

ALL WINTER LONG I heard stories about Jojo Mitewin, and at times I thought the storytellers might be putting me on. If they were, I never minded. The role of the naïve white guy had its advantages. The more gullible I sounded to them, the more they would lead me on with fantastic tales. One story went something like this:

"One night we was whoopin it up, an I says some things about Jojo. Next day I seen him here, I was sittin right here in the convent. He come in an give me the evil eye, ah? Then he's gone, Jojo. I says, 'What was that about, ah?'

'What was what about?'

I says, 'Didn't yiz see him give me the evil eye?'

'See who? We didn't see no one.' "

The Cree are great raconteurs. They are comparable to people like me, roughly speaking, as the Irish are to the English. They have the gift of the gab and a great abundance of humor. I think this gift must come from an age-old tradition of stories around a fire or a kitchen stove during the long winter nights.

Jojo Mitewin was said to have a great sense of smell. He could get downwind from a bog or a thicket or a stream bed and tell what was up ahead where the bush was thickest. Was it a bear? A moose? A pair of denning wolves? Jojo could sniff the air and tell you. He would walk on the forest floor as though he were on skis in powder snow or as though the moss came up to meet his boots and cushion the sound of his approach. He didn't stomp through the bush; he glided. His hearing was so acute that he could pick out the sound of a spruce grouse mincing through the grass a hundred feet away. He could walk nonstop for miles and miles and never break a sweat. He could go where the snowmobiles could not follow, and he never got lost, because how could you be lost in your own backyard?

Jojo the legend, Jojo the man. How much of this stuff was true? I knew I had to find out for myself. There was always a stretch before suppertime at the convent when I was neither grading papers nor talking with students. I found out from one of the women in my class where Jojo's shack was. She took me there, and we rapped on his door, but no one was home. I returned to the shack several times throughout the winter, but Jojo (the legend or the man) was never there. Sometimes, however, I saw fresh boot tracks or snowshoe tracks leading out into the forest.

When spring came and I had given my last class of the year, I had a final lunch with my students. It was April, almost time for the annual spring bear hunt. The icicles were dripping from the eaves of the convent, but the snow was as deep as ever. I told my students that I would return once more from Winnipeg to administer their finals to them. Could someone, I pleaded, introduce me to Jojo Mitewin?

"No problem," said Elvis Roy.

Elvis was a quiet, thoughtful fellow a bit older than me who had a trapline that began just north of the town dump. No problem, said his friend Adam, who hunted with Elvis every fall. When their finals were over, they told me, they would go find Jojo and bring him to me. I don't think I quite believed them, but still, I could hardly wait.

When I flew in for the very last time, the snow was melting fast, the roads were rutted and filled with deep puddles, and the ditches that ran beside the town's few streets were all running with meltwater. In spite of the muck, it was a beautiful time for getting out and going for a walk. The big lake beside the convent, however, was still frozen solid.

Adam and Elvis came to me with a proposition. They couldn't find Jojo in the usual places, but they knew where he was going. He would be easy to find because every spring he hunted in the same valley, and it wasn't far from the town.

"You mean we have to trail him through the snow?" I said.

"Oh, no," said Adam, "we got wheels, man. We'll drive right to the valley. We got it all organized."

Adam was a great organizer. He had political leader written all over him. He was handsome and charismatic and a bit of a bullshitter, but a *likeable* bullshitter.

Adam dressed me up in a yellow Ski-Doo suit and Sorels, and away we went in Elvis's half-ton. We were a jolly crew. We took the road past the dump, bouncing along and spraying the trees on either side with water from the puddles. We came around a corner, and Elvis slammed on the brakes.

"You see what I see?" he said to Adam.

They leapt out of the cab. I clambered out after them and went around to the back of the truck. The men were loading their rifles and squinting into the bush on one side of the road. Some wide, fresh tracks seemed to lead away from the road and into the trees. Elvis beckoned me to return to the cab, and Adam climbed into the box with his rifle. Elvis threw it into first and drove slowly down the road. He asked if I would hold his rifle and hand it to him if he had to leap out of the truck.

"Is it a bear?" I said.

"Might be a bear," he said, glaring into the bush and glancing back at Adam, who was standing at the ready with his legs wide apart in the box of the truck like a man riding shotgun in an old Western movie.

"Might be a moose."

Elvis grinned at me. "Shoot first and ask questions later, ah?"

I think he was kidding. Elvis had always been such a quiet, thoughtful student—almost grave. But today he was anything but grave; he was positively gleeful. I had the feeling that we were no longer in my classroom. The truck poked along, in and out of a series of huge puddles, Elvis holding the wheel with one hand and peering into the bush. The truck seemed to know which way to go, because Elvis rarely had his eyes on the road. We came to a fork, where the road continued north, and the other road, more a trail than a road, headed back northeast at a sharp angle and up a long hill.

Elvis poked his head out the window and yelled to Adam, "You stay here. I'll drive up the trail and raise some hell."

Like a soldier at the Normandy landing, Adam vaulted out of the truck and into the puddles and took his place behind a fallen spruce. Here he could watch both roads and, if he had to, duck behind the fallen tree or use it as a gun rest.

Elvis gunned it up the hill about two hundred paces or so. First he looked back at Adam, who waved to him from a crouch; then he took the vehicle off the trail and into the bush along a smaller trail where the going was good. He stopped the truck and waited until all was silent. Then he clapped the palm of his hand on the horn and blasted away. It sounded like a giant saxophone stuck in the key of E. Elvis opened the door of the cab and I handed him his rifle. He waded into the bush in his galoshes, which were unzipped down to the bottom. Elvis's galoshes were always unzipped. He went no more than a dozen steps into the bush and waited. Then he raised his rifle up to the treetops and fired several times. We remained silent for a minute or so.

A shot rang out, and a distant voice growled, "Son of a bitch!"

We got back into the truck and drove back to get Adam.

"Moose got lucky today," Adam said. "Cow with a little one."

"Are you going after them?" I said.

"In there?" said Adam. "You drive a truck in there, how far you gonna go, ah?"

I had meant on foot, but I didn't want to push things.

We went back up the long hill, past where Elvis had stopped to honk his horn and fire his rifle, and continued up over the hill and down into a valley. The road had become one vast brown puddle, and Elvis's truck seemed to swim through it. We churned through canyons of muddy water and rose and fell in our seats, but Elvis's truck never faltered. At last we pulled off the road and stopped. The two men went to the back of the truck and began to set up a ramp for their snowmobiles. One was a big yellow affair, which I would ride on behind Adam, and the other was a small black machine with a cracked housing, which Elvis would drive to lead the way.

"Jojo's got a little cabin in there," said Adam. "He goes out from the cabin."

And we were off. I'm sure these snow machines could go slowly, but today my friends were clearly not there to look at scenery. We were all demons for speed, and we flew along a trail at the edge of a long cutline. *Come on, Adam,* I wanted to say. *Fess up. Jojo is a figment of your imagination. When we get to the cabin, I will enter and every student in English 100 will leap up and cry out "Surprise!" and the party will be on.*

I was beginning to tire of my assigned role as the naïve white guy.

We arrived at the small cabin, and snowshoe tracks and boot tracks were all over the place. Someone had packed the snow down all around the cabin and into the bush a ways to the outhouse. Elvis knocked and called out Jojo's name, and we went inside, but no one was there.

"Let's go, cowboys," cried Adam, and we roared off into the woods, following a fresh snowshoe trail. We seemed to go a long way, several miles at least, before we stopped beside a steep incline that overlooked a stream. The ravine was stuffed with small trees and bush, like an elongated thicket that wound through the valley. The snowshoe trail went right down into the bush and crossed the stream and went up the other side. I could see where the snowshoes had done some sliding, because the downward tilt was about the angle of a very fast ski slope. There was no way in the world that these guys could take their machines down there, and I was relieved. My head was buzzing from the noise and the vibrations of the motor.

But I was wrong.

Elvis went first, straight down the hill. He simply crashed through a wall of willows and small spruce and onto the ice that covered the stream and up the other side. I could hardly believe my eyes.

"C'mon, cowboy," cried Adam. "Let's ride!"

I tried to disguise my reluctance and climbed aboard behind Adam. I remember carrying his rifle with one hand and clinging to his midsection with the other. He revved up his engine, and I bid goodbye to all I knew and loved, and we rocketed down the trail Elvis had carved with the treads of his snowmobile. Each time we struck a hump in the snow, I grunted, and as we approached the tangle of bush and trees below, my grunts became louder and louder. It was my way of pleading for my life without *seeming* to plead for my life. And then we crashed through the ice. The sudden halt launched me upward and into a deep cornice at the far edge of the creek. I must have been twisted around in midair, because I landed rump-first. I might have been in shock. I got to my feet, and my legs were shaking and my hands had gone clammy. But I was virtually unscratched.

The rifle was still in my hands.

Adam was cussing and bleeding from the head and soaking wet from the thighs down. He was directing all of his venom at the great yellow snowmobile amid the gurgling of the stream and a roar from above. The roar was coming from our co-conspirator, Elvis, who was laughing maniacally.

Hauling the snowmobile out of the stream was not easy. We all tried to get a foothold on the ice and pull in unison, but the ice was cracking every which way, and the machine was upside down and seemed to be stuck on something under the water. But we got it out and hauled it back through the thicket, and there it stood, soaking wet with a bent runner and something wrong with the starter. Its housing was cracked just like the housing on Elvis's machine, and I wondered how many times they had practiced this maneuver. Adam and Elvis knew absolutely how to get the snowmobile started again and up the hill, but their methods differed, and a long discussion ensued.

I looked around and spotted the snowshoe track. It headed up the far side of the stream's bank on a relatively gentle slope not far from the place where Elvis's black snowmobile had climbed. I knew that we would be mucking around by the stream for some time, so I crossed over on the ice and stomped through the snow to see where the tracks led. I made it up the slope and looked back down at Adam and Elvis, who were still arguing about how to get the big expletive yellow snow-mobile started, and if that failed, how to get it up the expletive hill.

I wandered onto a trail, which became easier to follow, and soon I was walking almost comfortably in the steps of the alleged great hunter in snowshoes. When I returned in fifteen minutes or so, I would no doubt once again find my companions deep in discussion.

The trail wound pleasantly through the trees, and as the voices of my students faded, I found myself relaxing. The rays of the sun penetrated through the gloom of the forest, casting pale purple shadows of the trees on the snow. I heard a bird call, perhaps an owl, I don't remember. But I stopped to locate the bird up high and then lower, and then lower still until I was staring at a man I had never seen before. He looked like a vigorous old fellow, short and lean and almost too preoccupied to give me a second of his time. He wore a dark green parka, carried an old rucksack on his back, and held a bush rifle in one hand. He wasn't wearing any gloves.

"Jojo?" I said. "Jojo Mitewin?"

He looked at me with a blank expression, but beneath that blankness seemed to lie an attitude that I can only guess at. Was it disdain, plain and simple? Curiosity? Had he come back to see what the uproar was all about? Or was he just looking at me with indifference, the kind he might have felt for the countless people who talked about him and tried to roust him out of his cabin but were perhaps ill-equipped to understand him?

"Are you the hunter?" I said.

God only knows what I looked like to him. A tourist, perhaps, or a would-be disciple? One of those white men who were always asking questions of Aboriginals in worshipful tones? An intruder?

I realized before he turned away that he was not going to answer me, that he was going to walk into the bush in his snowshoes and disappear as though he had earned the right to be free from people like me.

And that's just what he did. *There goes the last great hunter,* I said to myself. *The last great hunter.*

HUGH BRODY TELLS us, in *The Other Side of Eden,* that "there are virtually no people in the world today who live purely as hunter-gatherers." Loss of habitat is one obvious reason for this decline among hunters. Loss of habitat, loss of wildlife. Brody has dedicated his life to studying Aboriginal hunter-gatherers throughout the North. He managed to learn some of their languages and became intimate with their ways. I torture myself with the conviction that had Hugh Brody been there in the woods instead of me, he would have worn the proper footwear. He would have pursued Jojo Mitewin and befriended him.

Writers with Brody's dedication to the natural integrity of the wilderness and to the First Nations people who still live there bring back warnings for all of us. One of these writers is Rick Bass. He studied the migratory caribou up on the barren grounds. In his book *Caribou Rising,* Bass reminds us that the storied Porcupine herd of Arctic caribou has declined from 180,000 to

129,000 animals in less than two decades. Oil drilling in Alaska, espoused by the Bush-Cheney administration, could finish off this herd and the people whose culture and very survival depend on its health.

Change continents and we get roughly the same story; it scarcely matters which continent. Jerry Haigh has seen wildlife depredation and its impact on native hunters all over the world, and each of his observations falls into a similar story line. His experiences in Africa give us just one example.

Haigh was trained as a veterinarian in Glasgow, and East Africa was one of the remote places where he worked, observing and studying wildlife. He notes that the growth of human population in Africa exceeds that of any other continent. If the Pleistocene Africa, the land of abundant lions, rhinos, hippos, and elephants, is all but gone, it is because their habitat has turned, like the Great Plains of North America, into an agricultural and industrial landscape. The pressure to invade the last wild spaces comes, at one end, from a population of poor people trying to scratch out a living from the ground, and, at the other, from groups of landowners who are greedy for more land, more cattle, and the prestige that comes from it. In his most recent book, *The Trouble with Lions,* Haigh refers to this latter group of African land-owners as "megapastoralists."

In addition to this continental landgrab, local poachers prey on wild African animals for bush meat. Sometimes the simple need for food turns into a blood-bath, as it did in the Democratic Republic of Congo's

Virunga National Park, where the population of wild hippos plunged from 22,875 to 315 over a twenty-year period.

I can hear the irrepressible voice of Richie Goosen, booming with Alberta optimism through a megaphone: "No way in the world could we wipe out these critters."

I can hear the youthful voice of my friend Bill Watson saying, "Oh, yes we can."

"We" is not merely native poachers, squatters, ranchers, hunter-gatherers; it is the human race. In this massive kill-off, we are all complicit, and North America is part of a larger picture. North American history bears witness to the doomed hunt that used to sustain a vast network of First Nations people. From the North American Arctic and sub-Arctic hunters to the hunter-gatherers of the Great Plains as far south as northern Mexico, a tragic story unfolded in which subsistence hunting was pushed to the margins.

From the seventeenth to the nineteenth century, along the rivers where European traders met with Aboriginal hunters, primarily on the north side of the Medicine Line, the fur trade flourished. On the south side of the Medicine Line, the buffalo trade on the Great Plains took off. Subsistence hunting and trapping turned, of necessity, into commerce. Inevitably, from this point onward, the numbers of bison and fur-bearing animals began to decline.

Louis Bird, a Swampy-Cree elder and oral historian, mulls over an old complicity between Euro-Canadian traders and Aboriginal hunters. (He speaks to Roland Bohr, a historian who records him on tape.) When

Indians and Whites got into business, Bird tells us, both sides got greedy, and the old beliefs about the conservation of animals, the veneration of animals, were forgotten. When Christianity arrived among the Swampy-Cree, the priests "eliminated the traditional First Nations beliefs and practices. All the spiritual ideas were condemned and eliminated by 1950 . . . the code of ethics that was there in the minds . . . of people has been distorted and been sort of erased in the minds of the new generations . . ."

Since the days of massive erasures of Aboriginal culture in North America, there has been a cultural rebirth, from tribal group to tribal group, across the continent. Former victims of residential school abuse in Canada have taken part in a massive healing project, which has become one of the dramatic stories of our time. I've been learning about this story from a Saskatoon elder, an Ojibway counselor and spiritual leader by the name of Walter Linklater.

Walter was born and raised, until the age of seven, at the Couchiching First Nation north of Fort Frances, Ontario. His people were hunters and trappers, and each fall, young Walter would head up north to the family trapline and stay there with his parents in a small cabin all winter. This life ended for him when he was taken away from his parents and forced to go to a residential school.

Walter spent many years trying to recover his memory of his language (Anishinabe) and his family's practices. He had been told at the school, where he converted to Catholicism, that his parents were pagans, atheists, animal worshippers. But by talking to the old people about the years he was a child, Walter discovered that his parents were very spiritual beings. On mornings before a hunting and trapping expedition, the women would arise with the dawn and begin their prayers. These prayers came as they lit the morning fires and prepared the early-morning meal. Then the men would get up, and they too would sing their prayers. These prayers gave voice to their respect for the Earth, their Mother, and the Great Spirit. They would pray that the animals would be sent to the hunters to feed the people.

They had strict rules about overkilling, and if the day started off with an easy kill, the men would return early from the hunt. Walter remembers a particularly lucky day, on which the men brought down a moose at first light, and he watched them from the doorway of his parents' cabin as they returned on snowshoes over the early snow.

His people had been deeply spiritual from time immemorial. This discovery was a huge surprise to Walter. With help from the elders he began to remember the hunting rituals. Before a hunt, for example, the men would light a smudge from sweetgrass or some other plants, and they would take the smoke to their firearms to purify them before the kill. The animals were as much a part of their families as their own people, so to hunt them without reverence would be unthinkable.

*Totemtik.* This is a Cree word that Walter gave me so that I might understand this reverence for the animals. "*Totemtik* means all my relations, human and other." He does not have dominion *over* the animals; he is *connected* to them as though they were family.

I confessed to Walter that I had been a keen hunter in my time. I asked him something about the word *hunting*, the fact that Native subsistence hunters and sport hunters used the same word. Did that mean that some vital connections might exist between the two groups?

He didn't really answer the question, or perhaps his answer got lost among the many other questions I peppered him with. But one phrase remains in my taped interview with Walter that tells me what his people thought of white men who hunted for sport. "They killed animals just for the fun of it." As he said this, Walter's tone was closer to bemusement than moral disapproval. He seems to have left his youthful anger behind.

IF WE LOOK at Aboriginal hunting free of the constraints of commerce, free of the traders' greed and the greed of the hunters themselves, we can perhaps appreciate what Louis Bird meant, what it was like among the Native subsistence hunters of the North. Hugh Brody is helpful here. He strives, with admirable insight, to enter the Aboriginal hunter's psyche, including many of its cultural variations in various parts of the world. In this case, he speaks of the hunters of the Dunne-za First Nation (the Beaver Indians), who live at the Halfway River Reserve in the foothills of the northern Rockies.

The Dunne-za, like many other hunter-gatherer peoples, use dreams to locate both the animals they will kill and the routes along which they must travel to find these animals. The hunt is something other than mere hunting; rather, it is part of a vitally important relationship. The people depend upon the animals and the animals allow themselves to be killed. An animal's agreement to become food is secured through the respect that hunters and their families show to the land in general and to the animals in particular. If animals and hunters are on good terms, then the hunters are successful. If they are on bad terms, the hunt fails, and the animals withdraw into secret and unhappy places.

Brody talks with these hunters and hunts alongside of them. He learns how to connect the dreams with the specific techniques of the hunt. "To find the animals that are willing to be killed, Dunne-za hunters travel along trails that reveal themselves in dreams." This seems to be the only way that the hunters can enlist the voluminous amounts of information about their home territory in the cause of hunting success. "Dreaming," Brody reminds us, "is the mind's way of combining and using more information than the conscious mind can hold. It allows memory and intuition and facts to intermingle."

In North America, we have two historical traditions of hunting, then, and these systems are at odds with one another. The sport hunters gather in friendship and manliness, or in Artemisian solidarity, to feel more completely alive. The animals are there for their diversion. The subsistence hunters, women included, gather to feed their families as they have always done. The animals are likened to blood relatives of the tribes that hunt them. In both cases, the hunt has become an age-old source of cultural reaffirmation, but the two cultures seem resolutely opposed to each other's rights to hunt and to their practice of hunting.

And the two traditions have become splintered over the last half-century or so. Legions of sport hunters have stopped being sporting about the hunt. They let their ATVs, their expensive toys, their guides, or their money do the hunting for them. And many Aboriginal hunters have lost the tradition of spirituality that guided them in their prehistoric hunting days. Trevor Herriot puts it this way: they "no longer follow dream trails or anoint their rifles or live in that matrix of respect, reverence and relationship that the elders speak about."

What can Aboriginal subsistence hunters of conscience learn from the entreaties of conservation-minded sport hunters, and what can these sporting hunters learn from the time-honored beliefs of Aboriginal hunters? A common criticism from sportsmen in North America is that Native hunters don't observe any seasons or bag limits. They will shoot a pregnant cow moose or a bearing caribou as readily as a bull. They will, even today, kill whales, which are clearly endangered animals.

There is another side to this story. If, for example, we listen to what Native caribou hunters tell us about their hunting beliefs, we can discover signs of reticence and even compassion toward these animals. Here is the voice of Mathieu Mestokosho, describing a winter caribou hunt in Labrador. He was a great Innu hunter in the early twentieth century, and his stories of the hunt were translated from his Algonkian tongue to French and then into English:

We had just finished our work when the old hunters arrived with the caribou fetuses, which they
laid in the middle of the tent . . . After the meal,
my grandfather picked up the rope that had been
tied to one of the caribou fetuses and asked the
other hunter seated by him, "What was the rope for,
since we had bags to carry the fetuses?" The others, who were seated in two rows, each facing the
other, replied that it wasn't them. "Well, who then?"
demanded my grandfather. And Puniss replied, "It
was me and there's no point talking about it any longer." But my grandfather snapped back that he must
know that no one has the right to transport a caribou fetus without carrying it in a bag. "We will have
a cold north wind because of your error. We aren't
very well sheltered from the wind here. It's [like] a
desert."

Puniss said to my grandfather, "I didn't want to
stain my coat with blood." Puniss was wearing a
white coat that he wanted to keep clean.

Here are hunters on snowshoes, already overbur-
dened with supplies, who nevertheless carry with them
the fetuses of all the bearing cows they have shot, as
though they are bearing the weight of their transgres-
sions against the caribou, carrying their remorse upon
their backs.

Mestokosho and his fellow hunters shot thousands
of caribou over half a century ago to feed their families.
If they didn't succeed in killing a lot of animals, they
knew that they ran the risk of not making it through

the winters. They hunted on foot, trailing the herds of caribou. They walked astounding distances in the snow. They sometimes used dogs to help pull their equipment on toboggans, but they did most of the work without dogs. They lived through the coldest winters in tents. It was a life that allowed no laziness or any kind of slacking. They never talked about habitat or species conservation, but Mestokosho's people grew up with cautionary stories about hunters who went too far and killed too many caribou. Mathieu Mestokosho never resorted to surveys or statistics to back up his claims of excessive hunting; instead, he told morality tales of people starving the following winter because they could no longer find any caribou.

HUNTING SEASONS. Bag limits based on surveys. Laws that dictate which species and which sex can be killed and when it is legal to kill them. Specific hunting and no-hunting zones. Conservation officers. These are the constraints I grew up with as a hunter. We tried to obey all the regulations because if we got caught by a game warden (as we called them in the early days), we would be fined and our guns would be taken away. But I honored these regulations, and I still do, and not just to avoid the penalties.

The system I grew up with was geared toward controlling nature. The areas prescribed by law where hunters can pursue wildlife are called management zones. The system that governs these laws is called wildlife management. It's the white man's way. I honor this system, but I'm not entirely comfortable with the assumptions that come with it, especially the belief that we can control nature.

We fill the new land with our offspring and subdue it and have dominion over the fish of the sea and over the birds of the air and over every living thing that moves upon the earth. If a wave of prosperity dictates that we need, say, three new strip malls, an expanded suburb, two golf courses, and a bigger drag-racing facility, we feel entitled to destroy all the habitat we require for the new projects. When someone questions these actions, we remind her that this is progress and no one with any brains will mess with progress. Genesis 1, verse 28, run amok.

Mathieu Mestokosho will tell us of poor hunting practices among his own Innu hunters, men who waste meat, men who leave dead caribou to rot because the hunters are too tired to retrieve and butcher the animals. My father talked about some of his own hunting companions in the same way. Is it too much of a stretch, then, to say that the failings of hunters, both Aboriginal and non-Aboriginal, are pretty much the same thing? Surely a coalition of concerned sport hunters and hunter-gatherers would agree that decisions on the future of hunting in North America should have a lot more to do with the health and abundance of the animals and a lot less to do with anyone's right to harvest them. It all starts, as Trevor Herriot keeps reminding me, with the three Rs: reverence, respect, relationship.

Am I dreaming here? Could such a coalition of Aboriginal and non-Aboriginal hunters ever exist?

Would they ever sit down and agree that what's good for the ecosystem and the wildlife is good for all of us? Dreamy-eyed idealists all? When you read luminaries like Hugh Brody and Ted Chamberlin and Barry Lopez, you come to believe that such miracles of solidarity are possible.

In the spring of 2008, my brother sent me an article by Elie Dolgin about the Dolly Varden. The Dolly is a tasty char freckled with small pink dots on its side and beautifully white-edged fins, and it has always been very popular with anglers in British Columbia. It was named after a character in a Dickens novel who was fond of polka-dotted calico. Like their cousins in Alberta, the bull trout, the Dolly Varden in the Yukon and Northwest Territories were suddenly placed on the endangered list. Biologist Nathan Millar was assigned the daunting task of locating one of the Dolly's most vital spawning grounds so that he could implant the adult fish with radio transmitters and follow their progress as they migrated upriver. His research could provide fisheries biologists with the necessary information to try to save the species. But after much searching along the Vittrekwa River, he managed to find almost no fish for tagging.

In desperation he turned to his Native assistant for help. Stephen Tetlichi, a traditional hunter from the area (Fort McPherson), took Millar to his uncle, an elder named William Teya. This uncle remembered a time when the Gwich'in people could count thousands of Dollies in their spawning streams. The problem was that the last time William Teya had visited the spawning grounds of the Vittrekwa River was over fifty years ago, and back then the best way in was by dogsled.

With a mixture of skepticism and desperate hope, Millar loaded Teya into a helicopter, and they both began to search the river for signs of the spawning ground. The search took only minutes. Because of William's great intimacy with the places in which he used to hunt and fish, he led the team right to the spot. The Gwich'in people and the fisheries biologists had an equal stake in the health of this creature, and so they cooperated to the great fortune of the Dolly Varden.

This success story is merely my most recent example of hunter-gatherer nations cooperating with white conservationists to protect wildlife from extinction. A fuller account of this kind of cooperation can be found in Ian McAllister's recent book, *The Last Wild Wolves,* in which a young white scientist, Chris Darimont, teams up with an elderly tracker, Chester Starr, a mixed Heiltsuk and Kitasoo native, who is also a trained archaeologist. Together they track and study wolves in an attempt to protect the remaining packs of the Great Bear Rainforest. The cooperation between such disparate peoples feels like a form of ecumenicism among different religions.

Writer Barry Lopez reminds us that traditional hunting peoples all over North America cleave to the notion that "a spiritual landscape exists within the physical landscape." His initial source for this observation was a Lakota woman named Elaine Jahner. From time to time, the hunter would see something "fleeting in the land, a moment when line, color, and movement intensify and something sacred is revealed, leading one to believe that there is another realm of reality corresponding to the physical one, but different."

The corresponding hunting orthodoxy that has descended to me from its origins in the British Isles and its early North American adherents (Henry David Thoreau's *Walden*, for example) is a mix of transcendentalism, which sees the sacred in the natural world, and ethical thinking that derives from western philosophy. The hunters I know, atheists though some of them may be, are in many cases willing to talk about the wilderness and its creatures in sacred terms. Hunters of good conscience from all over the continent, white or Aboriginal, seem to understand these days that if hunting, under the pressures of farming in the South and mining and drilling in the North, were to become a thing of the past, an entire mosaic of complex and intelligent cultures would surely go down with it.

My own hope is that this complex of beliefs handed down from older to younger hunters will in some way be preserved and that it will inform our future relationship with wild animals and the habitat that sustains them. As I've intimated earlier in this chapter, I am always looking for signs that enlightened First Nations hunters, and the enlightened ones from my own tribe are viewing the hunt with a similar kind of reverence and respect. Sometimes I don't have to look very far.

Karla Jessen Williamson, a respected scholar, is a *kalaaleq* (an Inuk from Greenland) who married a white man and moved to Canada. She had grown up on a diet of wild meat—caribou, auks, eiders, seal and whale meat, as well as cod, red snapper, salmon, and char. She never hunted out on the ocean for whales or out on the ice for seals, because these hunts were done by the men. But during the summers around the fjords in southwest Greenland, Karla hunted for caribou with her family to supplement the food that they bought from the store.

In her new home in Saskatchewan, she generally adapted well—she was linguistically gifted, and she had all the intellectual stimulation she wanted. But she had to adjust to pork, pizza, chicken, and other types of perplexingly domestic fare that she purchased at malls in Saskatoon. When Karla shopped for food at Safeway, she used to bring her daughter, Laakkuluk, along with her. When Laakkuluk was three years old, she beheld an impressive array of meat on the counter one day. She turned to her mother and said, "Safeway must be a very good hunter!"

Karla soon became desperate to eat *real food*. She was fortunate to meet people in Saskatoon who were ardent hunters, and two of her favorites were Barbara and Ruthanne Hanbidge, whom we met in Chapter 6. They took her out deer hunting in some of their best-loved spots, and the three women did very well in the venison department.

They might have had different motives for hunting—the Hanbidges for recreational reasons and Karla for cultural ones—but they bonded during these outings. This bonding was possible, Karla claims, because all three women brought the same degree of reverence and respect for the wild animals. "Their intentions were right," Karla told me. "When you hunt and kill an animal for food, your intentions must be right." The three women felt a sort of "unquestioned bonding" because they shared a set of values toward the habitat, the game laws, and the animals themselves. "We could all feel connected to the animals and to the land." The Inuit never shoot an animal if they have a poor chance of killing it. To cause suffering for an animal would be unthinkable. The Hanbidge women agree heartily.

One of Karla's only surprises at hunting with Ruthanne and Barbara was on the question of sharing meat. In Greenland, when Karla brought down a caribou, she always shared the meat with the families of all the people on the hunt. But when she hunted with the Hanbidges and brought down a deer, they gave her their blessing to keep all of the meat herself. As she had done with the caribou in her native Greenland, she would bring the carcass right into the home and butcher it there rather than doing it outside or in a gutting shed.

I was impressed with the gravity in Karla's voice when she spoke about bringing death to a wild animal. This feeling applies equally to the land and to the plants that grow on it. "When you snap off a pea pod or a bean to eat, it is the same snap of death an animal might feel when you break its neck." There is no essential difference. The women's relationship with the land and with the animals must be sound, even if the women do less actual hunting than the men. The men depend on the women's compassion.

I feel lucky that hunters like Karla Jessen Williamson and Walter Linklater were patient enough to further my education on the subject of Aboriginal hunting, an education that must have begun with my failed conversation with Jojo Mitewin. Sometimes it feels as though I am still on his trail.

Jojo, wherever you are, come back and talk to us.

# 8 PLEASURE

*Alertness: the hunter is the alert man.*
JOSÉ ORTEGA Y GASSET, *Meditations on Hunting*

IN THE late 1960s and early 1970s, I usually shot to get my limit of grouse or mallards. On a good day, my friends and I would come home with whatever the limit allowed. On a rare day, I would fill out my own limit and help my hunting partners fill theirs. As a bird hunter I was so keen for the kill that I would sometimes have to force myself to walk more slowly so as not to elbow my buddies out of my way and get off the first shot. I wanted to return to the car with the pockets of my hunting coat bulging with birds. Like Hemingway, I wanted to kill cleanly, often, and in a way that gave me pleasure and pride. If, by the end of the day, I had shot badly, I would try to prolong the hunt and shoot at one more bird, and then another, until it was dark. The drive home was usually depressing.

During this time, I had a recurrent dream. I am hunting with a friend, and we have shot some birds. A sort of frenzy has taken over, and as the dream reaches its climax, we have cornered some grouse in an old barn. They try to hide in the stalls, and we blast them. They fly like pigeons up to the rafters, and we blast them. The remaining birds try to hide in my room, behind my desk, and under the bed. I crawl along on my belly like a trooper, and as they come out from under the bed, one by one, I line up the grouse and shoot them until the last bird is gone.

Well, I warned you that you'd get confessions.

This recurrent dream came around the same time (1972) that I began to phase out my hunting. I did not return to the field for many years. It is difficult for me to explain this prolonged lapse in my hunting life. The pleasure in the hunt declined as my guilt about killing increased, and my recurrent dream was a measure of this guilty feeling.

But I wonder if, back in the days of the Wild West, those men who shot all those buffalo from sidecars and wagons and left them to rot—if they too had these remorseful dreams. I wonder if the men who shot thousands and thousands of great auks and passenger pigeons and whooping cranes for the so-called sport of it had dreams like mine.

What is always missing from my dream of slaughter is the pleasure of the hunt. As a young man, when I shot to get my limit, too often the excitement was great but the pleasure was shallow, a satisfaction that sank only as deep as the ego. Shooting to get my limit was like drinking to get drunk. I was an avid hunter of pheasant, grouse, and mallards, but as we shall see, my greatest pleasures in the field were still ahead of me.

My resumption of hunting came in the fall of 1986. I wanted to bring Raymond Carver up to Saskatchewan to do a public reading, but the English department where I taught could not afford him. Knowing that Carver had once been a keen hunter, I promised him a plane ticket and a goose hunt. His only condition was that he be allowed to bring Richard Ford with him. I could scarcely believe my luck: Carver was the working-class hero of American fiction, and Ford was America's young novelist on the rise.

I brought three buddies along for the ride—Bill Robertson, Bob Calder, and Peter Nash. Of the three friends, at that time, only Nash was an experienced hunter, but the six of us had a high old time. The weather was foul, the shooting was difficult, but the camaraderie was fine. That trip must have reminded me that great hunting had very little to do with getting my limit.

Richard Ford writes with real enthusiasm about the hunt in his essay "Hunting with My Wife." Hunting, he says, "requires avidity, a continual, alert responsiveness to the particulars of the changing situation you're in. Writers celebrate hunting so often partly because such exquisite, tuned readiness is not usual in life and can make one feel (though not write) like a romantic poet, which some people seem to want to be." Ford has put his finger on something that at least my own generation cries out for: hunters want the rush that comes with feeling fully and vibrantly alive, and this is why Ford fixes on the keen compulsions of romantic poets and hunters. "Most hunters know this avidity," he tells us. "Its evidence lies not in how well or fast you shoot, not how often you hit what you mean to, not even how quickly your gun comes to your shoulder, but how widely you see, how promptly you pick up a soft wingbeat and by its sound know it to be a hen's before you even see the colors. It is how quick you are to know that your young dog has lost a scent, and to find the bird yourself; then get your dog to refind it. It is concentration upon all the particulars of *one thing*, which is exhilarating and rare in life."

Trevor Herriot thinks of this avidity as a quasi-mystical state of mind. "A rock-climber, a tightrope walker, a parachute jumper" can all participate in the "mindfulness in what some have called a flow-state," where we focus for the duration of our experience "on immediate and unmediated experience." Neither José Ortega y Gasset nor Richard Ford would talk about the intense pleasure of hunting in this way. Ortega y Gasset would even refuse to call it pleasure. But it's clear to me that all three writers are onto something universal here, even though the ways in which they come to terms with it are wildly dissimilar.

IN SEPTEMBER OF 1989, I was having lunch with Richard and Kristina Ford at a Lebanese place in downtown Saskatoon. It was two or three years after the hunt we had had with Ray Carver, and Ray had been dead for about a year. A friend of Honor's and mine at the table brought the conversation around to hiking trails in Banff and Yoho.

I turned to Richard and Kristina.

"You two should come up here and do some hiking."

"Oh no, David," said Richard. "When I go for a walk in the woods, something has to die."

Round of laughter. This was one of those Ford moments of hyperbolic glee that gets recounted around here to this day. But his words made me wonder about the hunt. Could you go out hunting and not kill anything, time and time again, and still call yourself a hunter? I think the answer is no, but I'm still not sure.

I was beginning to withdraw from something in my own hunting life: the moment of the kill. I was still keen to go out but somehow, perhaps like Roderick Haig-Brown, less intent on shooting.

My hunting partner at this time was Doug Elsasser, and his specialty was whitetail bucks. Doug and his wife, Barb, live in the midst of some of the finest whitetail hunting in North America. In three decades of hunting, Elsasser has probably never known a bad deer season. From spring into late summer he watches the animals as they feed at the edge of his fields and the abundant meadows. When the rut arrives and the bucks get distracted, he chooses his day, gets up around six in the morning, has his breakfast, and simply walks out into the woods with his gun. He rarely sees another hunter.

It was my great luck to be one of his hunting partners from the mid-1980s to the mid-1990s. I would arrive in November when the first permanent snows had fallen and the tracking got interesting. When a fresh snow lies around you, naturally, all the tracks you see are fresh ones.

The night before we rose for one of our hunts, Doug was talking about a past encounter with a good buck. He and Barb and I were sitting by the wood stove just before bedtime. "I hear this clash and clattering sound somewhere below me in the valley. It's the sound of two bucks in rut fighting over the does. I hear the end of the fight, which means that one buck will stay and one will slink off into the woods. I catch a glimpse of the loser away below me with his head down, and I have to figure which way he'll go. It's like I'm almost asking him which one of three trails he'll take to get back up the hill and meet his fate. I choose the one on the far left and position myself there to wait. Sure enough, he comes up the trail toward me and I shoot him. How much more spiritual can it get?"

Elsasser seems to echo the words of Hugh Brody (*Maps and Dreams*) and Robert Brightman (*Grateful Prey*) when they speak of how the hunted animals die at the hands of their pursuers. If the hunters are on good terms with the big animals they hunt for their survival, if they honor their presence, the animals in turn will present themselves to the hunters as food. If the hunters dishonor the great animals (hunting to excess; hunting from all-terrain vehicles, trucks, or snowmobiles; showing indifference toward the dead prey), the hunt will go badly.

I'm not saying that lazy hunters who shoot from the cab of a half-ton don't get their animals. They do. I'm talking about a perception among pure and dedicated hunters. When I talk about this inherent spirituality among hunters, this intense relationship between the animals and their pursuers, I tend to sound flaky. I can report these beliefs to others, but Elsasser lives them. Brody and Brightman are talking about Aboriginal hunters, of course, but among hunters like Doug Elsasser is a strong spiritual element to their pursuit of the animals.

This angle of mine doesn't sound exactly macho, does it? When I read about sport hunting these days, all too often I get a different take on big-game hunters. Here is an example.

Susan Bourette makes a pilgrimage to find the perfect meat for foodies everywhere to consume. In her book, *Carnivore Chic,* she flees to Newfoundland, where she goes on a moose hunt. She is a sophisticated big-city writer whose visit to a hunting lodge feels like a voyage to the heart of darkness. Here is her take on Ted Nugent, the "most recognizable face of hunting in America." She is referring to two of his books, *Blood Trails: The Truth about Bowhunting* and *Kill It and Grill It!* "Nugent makes no bones about it—hunting is not only a primal act, but a sexual one: 'The heated excitement of the shot . . . the shaft was in and out . . . complete penetration . . . I was hot . . . I was on fire . . . the kill is climactic . . . it satiated a built-up frustration.' " Hunting for "the Nuge" is "an adrenaline rush."

The pleasure Elsasser experiences when he hunts cannot be confined to a rush of adrenaline or a fulfillment of his ego or a sexual conquest. It includes this strange (to outsiders) spiritual element unavailable to hunters who are not blessed with humility. And the pleasures of the hunt go well beyond what I have so far described. The best way to demonstrate this contention is to quit analyzing and get back to the hunt.

One of many hunts I had with Doug Elsasser was during a cold week in November of 1991. Before the sun was up, somewhere out in the darkness, the Elsassers' dog, Brewer, was barking at what sounded like a big old buck. It grunted back from somewhere down in the bottom land.

I was still half asleep and pondering how many layers to put on. If I dressed too warmly, I would sweat and then shiver in my sweat. Formula for pneumonia. If I dressed too lightly, the prairie wind could drift right through me, and I wouldn't last an hour out there. I pulled on my long johns and a thick pair of canvas hunting pants. On top I wore a T-shirt, a thick denim shirt, a wool sweater, a windbreaker with a hood, and a down jacket. Over all these clothes I wore my Day-Glo orange coveralls.

When we left the house, it was still dark outside, but the snow provided its own light. Our boots crunched along the trail and squeaked into the snow. We weren't up to much gabbing, and when we spoke it was in whispers.

"What do you have in that thing?" Doug said, pointing at my back.

We both carried day packs, but mine was considerably larger than his. It contained my lunch, a bottle of water, a small box of cartridges, an extra pair of socks, and some survival equipment that I'd never had to use—things I might need to filter water, for example, or signal a helicopter, or build an igloo.

"Stuff," I said.

The first whitetail buck I ever brought down was with Doug and his crew. It happened out here in

the Assiniboine River valley near the Saskatchewan–
Manitoba border on a warm November morning. The
deer in question was a youngish fat one with a broken
tine. They drove it out into the open and right across
my bow. It was too close for a scope, but I had my 30/30
with the peep sights. I simply raised my gun and fired,
and the deer went down with a shattered spine. I ran up
to it, raised my gun and fired again, dispatching it with
a head shot.

What I remember best about that day was the heart-
thumping excitement of it and a strange mix of elation
and regret. I could share the elation with Doug and
his friends as they gathered around to congratulate me
on my first whitetail, but I had no one I could talk to
about the regret. That was five years earlier. This time I
wanted to test myself to see if I could bring down a deer
and do so without regret. I wanted the excitement of the
hunt without the accompanying prick of conscience.

This morning there were no deer feeding in the first
meadow. None in the second meadow. The tracks we
found in the snow were yesterday's deer. We decided to
split up. Doug found some fresh tracks, and then more
fresh tracks, and in a state of great eagerness, he came
back to where I'd been marching through the knee-high
snow.

"Carp," he said, "remember that lower meadow on the
other side of the creek?"

I nodded in a vague sort of way. I thought I might
have known the meadow he was referring to. He continued to whisper as though the deer were eavesdropping,
and I could see his breath as the words came out.

"I'm going to walk a couple of miles along the upper rim of the valley and come back down again toward you. They'll probably catch my scent and come back this way through that meadow. You walk down to the meadow and find a good spot and wait for them to come through. I'll be a few minutes behind them."

Doug was determined that I would have the first shot of the day. He wanted me to go home with some venison; it was a generous plan. A moment later he was trudging uphill through the snow. While Doug headed to the northeast, I made my way along a path to the southeast. I walked into the meadow away ahead of schedule. It was small, shaped roughly like an oval, about the size of a high-school running track. It leveled out nice and flat in front of me, and the hills rose sharply up to the north and east. In less than half an hour Doug would be coming down through the trees toward me, making as much noise as he could.

I eased into some willows and began to shadowbox to keep warm. Not an easy thing to do with a rifle. I put down the rifle, leaning the barrel into the crotch of a large willow stump, and continued to throw hooks at Joe Frazier. I must have discovered at this point that I was George Foreman.

I really was looking for the first deer to cross the meadow, and I really was listening for Doug's approach. But all was quiet as I shadowboxed the unfortunate Mr. Frazier into a corner. Okay, I could have been quieter and more vigilant, but I needed to keep my blood pumping on account of the cold. I'm not a very good still-hunter; I need to be constantly on the move. I don't know how many minutes passed, but quite a few, when I heard Doug's voice, clear and distant and bellowing like a bull elk: "Carpenter, where the hell are you?"

When you are out in the woods, separated from your hunting partner by miles of bush and forest and hills, you will call out a message as brief and simple as possible. You don't mess around with extra verbiage. So when I heard the words "the hell" inserted into Doug's bellowed query, I knew that very second that I had stopped at the wrong meadow.

"Carrrr-penter, where the hell are you (*elll arrre youuu*)!"

His voice sounded as if it was coming from the northeast and well above me, perhaps a mile away. Where indeed was I? In a moment of genuine inspiration, I tore open my day pack and extracted a metallic blue object that looked like a small flashlight. I screwed in a red plastic charge about the diameter and half the length of my thumb. I raised the object to the sky, pulled back the spring-loaded button, and released it.

Elsasser must have heard the crack of the charge going off a second or so after he saw the rocket exploding above the highest grove of aspens and curving in a glowing pink trajectory, plunging to the earth like a fallen angel.

A second or two later, I heard some high-pitched laughter. And that, pretty much, was our morning.

AFTER OUR LUNCH in the bush, it turned colder. Doug decided to walk the coulees that come up from the river, and I walked the edge of the rim above him. All afternoon from the lake below, I heard the sound of shifting water beneath the vast long carapace of ice. Undulating lake water creates a continuous hollow sound like the vibes from a gigantic gong.

As the sun dipped closer to the horizon, I climbed down a ravine and got away from the wind for a while. At the end of the day, I climbed up to the steep rim of the Hills of Enlightenment, Barb Elsasser's favorite meditation roost. Down again. Passed through several meadows surrounded by big aspen woods. All up and down. Doug veered off through the Assiniboine Valley below. Alone, I saw three deer in three locations, but they were either too quick to run or already out of range.

It was very cold that day. In this weather, because my clothes were just right, I could walk twice as far and climb twice as well as I could on a warm day. Discovering such endurance is quite a feeling for a man well into middle age. It's a wonderful country that can make you feel strong and give you the gift of solitude. And a wonderful feeling to trudge back home to a warm cabin and the smell of food and Barb and Doug's stories of this lucky place.

WE AWOKE THE next day to the news on the radio that a storm was coming. Roy Elsasser, Doug's dad, dropped Doug and me off in his pickup. We headed southeast toward the rising sun, and as the clouds gathered before us, we pushed bush into a stiff, cold wind. Despite a certain loss of hearing, so important to a hunter, I had to pull down my earflaps and walk myself warm. I saw no deer but kept pushing bush with Doug always on my left. At last we came together and walked across the open pasture. I had gotten disoriented, as I regularly do in unfamiliar territory, and I was simply trudging along with Doug. The sun had completely disappeared behind the oncoming clouds, so which direction we were heading was anybody's guess.

At one point we stopped, and Doug observed a fenceline—*and he didn't recognize it.* We had been walking in and out of the bushes across the community pasture, changing directions frequently, and suddenly I thought, *we are lost.* I tried out my theory.

"Let's go," I said to Doug.

"Where?"

"Home," I said.

"We are going home."

"How do you know?" I said.

He didn't answer, so we went on in silence until at last he pointed to a small grove of spruce trees about a mile to the northeast.

"Those trees are in Fuzz's backyard," he said, referring to a neighbor I'd met some time ago.

I wanted to believe Doug, but what if he was wrong? How long would we last before the coming storm would drive us into the bush to escape the wind? In the bush you stay a bit warmer, but then *no one can find you.* And the storm really was coming, closer and closer.

But in spite of the washed-out light and the gray afternoon, Doug had seen something that looked familiar. The subtle contours and undulations of the land, the various copses we passed, had been enough to tell him just where we were. We weren't lost; we were less than a mile from Doug and Barb's cabin. We arrived home in the middle of the afternoon. As I wrote the notes in my journal that I eventually used for this story, I could feel how the prairie had scored my face red and raw. The big storm had arrived.

That afternoon I confessed to Doug that I'd been worried we were lost in the community pasture. Perhaps my worries weren't entirely misplaced. Later that day, one of Doug's friends, a farmer on a nearby section of land, asked us to hunt with him in the last two hours before nightfall. We left him as darkness was falling because he wanted to check out one last bush for a deer. His wife phoned us in the storm three hours later because he still hadn't returned. At last, around nine o'clock, he came in. He had gotten lost on his own land. Not a hard thing to do in a storm in bush country. There was something cold and menacing out there, and I was grateful *not* to be going outside to hunt for a lost hunter.

I WENT TO sleep that night to the moaning of the wind. I awoke once during the night, and the wind was still at it. Sometime after that, the wind had fallen, and in the morning we wandered from our bedrooms into the living room. We all looked out at the surrounding forest. The new snow was banked up against the house and the trees and the driveway, and the cornices had been teased and twisted into gestures that looked like the corniest of landscape canvases and the usual comparisons to whipped cream.

After breakfast, Doug and I walked up to the road that runs by his place, crossed it, and followed a trail

almost wide enough to be called a road. We took this
trail for a mile or more up to an ever-narrowing field surrounded by groves of twisted aspen. The field fell away
on both sides into big ravines, and at the far end of the
field, there was a good view below of the Assiniboine
Valley. The idea was to walk to the end of the field and
have a look down there for fresh tracks. But before we
could even enter the field, Doug spotted some whitetails browsing at the edge of the aspens, only three or
four hundred yards away. Luckily we had been walking into the wind, and the willows on both sides of the
trail had at least partially obscured us from the browsing
deer. Perhaps the deer could not even imagine hunters
out in the field right after such a horrendous storm. And
because we had walked, no sound of a vehicle would her-
ald our entrance into this snowbound habitat.

Through his scope, Doug glassed the herd and spotted a good buck, the lone squire of these does. We
stooped down and edged closer to the herd, the wind
muffling our approach. At last, Doug leaned his rifle on
a weathered old fence post, stood for a long time while
his breathing slowed and seemed to stop altogether, and
then he fired, twice. The trees sent back the twin reports
of his rifle, and the deer raised their astonished white
tails and bounded for the bush.

"I think I got him," said Doug.

"I didn't see anything drop," I said.

"Me neither," he said, "but I think I hit him good."

We marched across a harvested field of barley, heav-
ing our legs up out of the deep snow, laboring to get to
the deer as fast as we could. At the edge of the field I

spotted fringes of uncut barley drooping over the fresh snow. The deer must have sniffed these out.

"Carp, over here."

Doug's buck had managed to make it to the trees. It must have died seconds after Doug shot it, a big grain-fed four-pointer (what Americans refer to as an eight-pointer) with a partially healed scar over its right shoulder, perhaps from a fight with another buck. The animal was still young, but it must have weighed a good 250 pounds. We field-dressed it on the spot and stood over it while Doug said a few words, giving thanks to a pagan voice beyond the thunder that sent us snowstorms, cornices, and deer.

ALWAYS, EACH OF my hunts with Doug felt like an adventure. Even getting lost, to me, had a certain savor to it. We always brought down a deer or two, but the adventure started long before the first shot was fired. It started with the physical pleasure of it. I would begin each hunt by driving out of my city of 210,000 people surrounded by a suburb where the cars swarmed in and out like hornets. I would always have a salad or a light meal before I left, but by the time I'd reached the town of Kamsack, I was a hamburger-ravening beast who had forgotten his urban life, his daily regime with the laptop, his domestic routines with his family.

From the first morning out in the dark and the snow I would start to use my senses. At times, hearing could become more important than sight. The crack of a twig, an exhalation of breath, the soft concussion of hooves on snow—these sounds would help bring my eyes into play. I would even find myself from time to time using my nose in ways that surprised me.

The smallest detail out there in the quiet woods, like a shift in the wind or a broken branch, can be crucial. Each deer trail has its own mysterious narrative. If the back hooves land outside the front hooves, you probably have a doe, because her hips are proportionately wider than those of the buck. If the back hooves land upon, or inside, the front hooves, you probably have a buck. To be sure, you sniff around for patches of urine. The does pee a small neat hole in the snow. The bucks are messy pissers and send their urine all over the place, as though they are learning to do graffiti for the first time. The messier the job, the bigger the buck. Walk slowly and keep looking around you and up to the far horizon. Every once in a while, you will be rewarded with a good sighting.

On the hunt, you are leaving behind a mental existence, exchanging it for a physical, instinctual one. The miles that you walk go by, and you scarcely notice them, but as you call upon your body to take you up and down the ravines and through the deep snow, you cannot escape the profound pleasures of solitude and of encountering your own strength.

And always, as José Ortega y Gasset would say, there is that ever-present possibility of the "mystical union with the animal, a sensing and presentiment of it that automatically leads the hunter to perceive the environment from the point of view of the prey, without abandoning his own point of view . . . The pursuer cannot pursue if he does not integrate his vision with that of the pursued. That is to say, *hunting is an imitation of the*

182 · A HUNTER'S CONFESSION

*animal* . . . In that mystical union with the beast a contagion is immediately generated and the hunter begins to behave like the game. He will instinctively shrink from being seen; he will avoid all noise while travelling; he will perceive all his surroundings from the point of view of the animal, with the animal's peculiar attention to detail."

On the trip I was just recounting, I was discovering something else about myself. I had gone three days without firing a shot. Not an unfamiliar situation for me and my rifle. Doug tried more than once, on other occasions, to put me on point for a good shot, but of necessity he ended up doing all the shooting himself. At my most effective, I was his dog, his pusher of bush. And the pleasure from this encounter was much deeper than it would have been during my youthful days of weekend potting, frenzied driving at four in the morning, and limiting out.

I don't know why. Pleasure is easier to recount than to explain.

This pleasure, though, extends very nicely beyond the hunt. The planning and preparations carry their own kind of excitement. The stories of the hunt are sometimes so engaging that they last for decades after the hunt is over; they last and they grow, with appropriate hyperbole, until they become legends.

And then there is the eating. Yes, the eating.

IMAGINE, IF YOU will, a snowbound cabin in late November. Imagine several venison loins in a flat pan, awaiting your attention.

Imagine a bottle of white wine, and I don't mean your most coveted chardonnay. Just some plonk. Pour two cups of this wine into a bowl and mix in as much as a tablespoon of soy sauce and a healthy dash of Worcestershire sauce. Pour this marinade over the venison loins and leave the meat covered, overnight, in the pantry. In the absence of a pantry, any cool place will do.

Imagine that the next day is Sunday, and you and your hunting buddies can take it easy, do some exploring, but leave your guns in the cabin. The designated cook lifts the loins out of the marinade and is smart enough to avoid drinking it. He discards the marinade. He chops two or three onions, a couple of large cloves of garlic, and a bounteous double handful of mushrooms. Sautés the onions and garlic in butter and adds the mushrooms for the last two or three minutes of sautéing. He places these veggies in a bowl (drained of their butter). He grills the loins on the barbecue or in the oven, adding whatever seasoning he thinks appropriate. He opens a bottle of cabernet, summons the rest of you to the kitchen table, places the sautéed veggies on top of the meat, and serves.

You might be a grass-fed beef advocate, a vegetarian, a prime-cut meat snob, a devotee of strictly porcine pleasures, a lowbrow hamburger-and-fries lover, a bison buff. But once you've eaten your own venison with all the appropriate preparations and reverence, you might well become a true believer.

## 9 BLOOD

*'God save thee, ancyent Marinere!*
*From the fiends that plague thee thus—*
*'Why look'st thou so?'—with my*
*crossbow I shot the Albatross.*

SAMUEL TAYLOR COLERIDGE,
*The Rime of the Ancyent Marinere*

THE LAST grouse I ever took was killed on September 14, 1995—a spruce grouse, a lovely male with scarlet combs above the eyes. When I picked him up, he was bleeding from the beak, and because the blood had escaped from a lung shot, it bubbled out somewhere between blazing pink and bright red. I gutted and skinned the bird, boned it for a stew I was making, and with a certain woodsman's pride, awaited the arrival of my friends. They came in three vehicles, led by Bob Calder, my fishing buddy and the man who owned the cabin.

By the time the lot of us sat down to eat, it was dark. They liked my grouse stew, and I must have gone to bed with a satisfied smile. The grouse had been out in great numbers, ruffies and sharptails as well. It's not often we see so many grouse up north of Narrow Hills within a few miles of Bob's cabin. We had made a very nice start to our weekend.

The sound of a woodpecker awakened me early the next morning. I went into the kitchen to make coffee and get the fire going in the stove. With the aroma of fresh coffee curling through the cabin, Calder emerged from his bedroom. We decided not to hurry breakfast, to let our friends sleep in a bit. I left Calder to sip his coffee and bring in the morning. I walked down the road, hoping, I suppose, to see another grouse. I didn't have my shotgun with me, but I had my trusty rabbit stick. It's the length of my forearm and about as thick as the leg of a chair. I throw it low and parallel to the ground so that it spins like the blade of a helicopter. I could hear some drumming in the woods.

At this time I was recovering from an operation on my nasal passages. The surgeon had snipped off some polyps a way up into my nostrils, cut away some cartilage, widened both nostrils, and corrected the constriction in my beak—a common procedure, I am told. The following day I was sent home from the hospital and urged to take it easy for a couple of weeks.

Now here I was, two weeks later to the day, surrounded by trout ponds, grouse, and friends, listening to the frenetic rapping of a woodpecker. A pileated woodpecker, it turned out to be, a sort of chainsaw with feathers. He was sending the chips flying in his search for grubs and ants in a big rotting tree. He would occasionally send a sharp *kuk* to his mate and then continue dismantling the tree. As the Ancient Mariner did to the water snakes, I blessed him unaware. A kind of Aldo Leopold moment, I suppose. A kind of Bill Watson moment.

I walked away, still holding my rabbit stick, and the woodpecker called to his mate—*whucker whucker whucker*. Nature's great extrovert.

This role was familiar to me, the man who walks into the woods, bowing with reverence to the wonders of nature but carrying a weapon with deadly intentions. I needed to take a practice throw. I spotted a tree stump, reared back with my rabbit stick, and let it fly. It spun past my target, and I went to retrieve the stick. This journey led me into a large sand pit surrounded by black spruce. I scooped up some dried mushrooms and looked down to examine them. Suddenly there was a puddle of blood in my hand. In a second or two, as I flung the mushrooms away, I knew I had more than just a nosebleed. I jammed a tissue into my right nostril and headed back to Bob's cabin.

The walk was about 650 yards. The tissue seemed to have no effect in staunching the flow, and as I walked, I began to swallow a steady stream of blood. I dropped the rabbit stick on the front porch and walked into the cabin. Bob was sipping coffee and listening to the radio. Our friends were still fast asleep in the guest bedroom.

I said to Bob, "I think we've got a problem."

Two of our guests were Paul and Julie Bidwell. Paul was the chair of my English department. Julie was a nurse, and she had dealt with a lifetime of emergencies. She saw that I was having a bad bleed and went immediately from slumber to emergency mode. She got me to press down with a cool washcloth on the area where the blood seemed to be coming from. She put together an ice pack and applied pressure. The bleeding began to abate. I could tell because I was swallowing less blood. Paul came out of the bedroom, adjusting his clothes, and Julie went back in to get dressed. When she returned, she started phoning around and quickly discovered that up around our community of Little Bear Lake, there were no doctors or medical facilities. At last, Julie found a hospital in Nipawin that was open for business. It was about one hundred miles southeast of Little Bear Lake, and it had an ambulance that would meet us halfway.

A bad bleed seems to have its own agenda, its own unique set of vascular pressures. My bleed suddenly went into overdrive. It seemed to burst out of the pressure dam we had created for it and rushed down my throat as fast as I could swallow. I summoned Julie, and she urged Paul to get us on the road as fast as we could go.

I did not entirely get the point. I knew that this situation was serious, but I didn't know the medical reasons. When Julie and Paul helped me up from my chair, out of the cabin, and into the car, I protested that I could make it on my own. When Paul hit the highway running, I reminded him that we weren't in so much of a hurry that we had to speed.

He sped. My boss at work had become Jacques Villeneuve of Hanson Lake Road. Julie said nothing about this transformation, as if she concurred that speed was of the essence.

I tried to lighten the atmosphere.

"If we pass a church," I told them, "I want to say a Paternostril."

Paul did not slow down. It was a long hour.

What I wasn't quite getting was that if through excessive blood loss I happened to faint, I could drown in my own blood. Julie knew this, and she must have told Paul, because somewhere between the cabin and the highway Paul went from a concerned friend to a man with one thing on his mind: our rendezvous with the ambulance from Nipawin.

The blood began once more to flow down my throat. I must have begun to grasp, at least intuitively, the gravity of my situation. I flashed on the grouse I had killed the day before, the bright red blood bubbling from its beak. The blood that flowed from my own beak. Men who hunt for sport do not, as a rule, think this way, but I began to regret having taken the life of a wild and beautiful creature. Somewhere north of Smeaton, Saskatchewan, I sent up a prayer. *Get me out of this one, and I swear, I will never again shoot another creature.*

I had once been a good hunter, pursued wild game with real passion. And on the day I brought down my last grouse, I was still very keen for the hunt. That enthusiasm all ended abruptly. Just who exactly I prayed to, I am not sure.

A few miles north of Smeaton, we spotted the ambulance. I had swallowed more blood than I ever want to remember, and I had begun to lose feeling in my forearms and legs. I had no idea why I was losing feeling in these areas. On my way to the stretcher, I was genuinely wobbly on my pins. The ambulance crew lifted me straight into their vehicle and strapped me in with my head elevated.

Julie was relieved to find out that the ambulance personnel had a suction machine at their disposal. At the time, I was oblivious to the importance of this device— that if I were to lose consciousness, the attendant was equipped to revive me and prevent me from drowning in swallowed blood. Before the vehicle took off for the Nipawin hospital, the attendant gave me oxygen.

His name was Kevin. His main job, I see now, was to keep me from getting too worried, because if I panicked, my heart rate would increase and an excess of blood would be pumped through my veins and out the broken vessel. Kevin's conversation turned to hunting and fishing. If that was a ploy, it was a good one.

DR. MARTENS HAD been at the Nipawin hospital for scarcely one week. It was his first day off, but apparently (being on call) he was already attending to an emergency case just a few feet from where I lay. Around noon he began to check me over. He was a big man, younger than me, and dressed casually in a weekend shirt and jeans. He didn't look much like a doctor. Immediately Martens ordered an IV to help compensate for the blood I had lost. Once he had located my leak, he began the painful process of plugging it. First he installed an inflatable device known as a Foley catheter. Once it was inflated inside my nasal cavity, it began to cut off the various passages where blood could flow—to dam up my blood, in other words, and to force it to slow down and clot. The catheter hung from my nostril, I imagine, like a sort of elephant's trunk. Martens also ordered some narrow, tough surgical packing dipped in a saline adrenaline solution both to block and constrict the broken vessel. The more he tamped, the deeper the tape was lodged inside my nasal passages. I was given a shot of Demerol and admitted to a ward. The idea was to move around as little as possible. I whispered to Julie that if I didn't make it out of this bleed, I wanted her to tell Honor and our son, Will, that I loved them.

She nodded knowingly. My request was part of a rite that dying people perform before the great darkness descends, and she had seen it plenty of times.

My condition, as you can see, had become critical. Julie and Paul never left my side. A measure of the gravity of my situation was that when Julie took my hand to reassure me, I would not let go. I clung to her as though she were a secret source of life. My wife arrived with Bob Calder, and Paul briefed her about my condition before she entered my ward. Nevertheless, Honor was unprepared to see me with what looked like a beached jellyfish covering part of my face. For a terrible second, she thought it was some sort of deformity, but it was just a collapsed plastic bag with ice cubes and a washrag inside.

She and Calder and Paul and Julie remained in my room or just outside it, and much to my relief, the nurses allowed them to stay. This emergency unit had some of the friendly appeal of country hospitality.

My system was beginning to shut down and go into emergency mode. By now I had lost almost all the

feeling in my limbs. I could not move my bowels or uri-
nate. My bladder began to swell until, as we used to say
in simpler times, my back teeth were floating. I can try
to tell this story with a certain measure of humor, but at
the time there was nothing funny about the way I felt. In
spite of my fears of such devices of torture, I called for a
urinary catheter.

Martens was summoned, but unfortunately he was
attending to his case in the intensive care unit. The
blood had found an opening in my plugged nostrils. First
came a massive clot the size of a big leech worming up
my throat, then came the blood under terrific pressure.
I gulped and gulped and then, for the second time that
day, I sent out a prayer.

I know. There are no atheists on a sinking ship. But
when you've resorted to all the usual avenues from medical cures to health insurance, and you're quite plainly
headed for the last roundup, you turn to the last resort,
the most entirely irrational one.

I looked up at the people in the room, and I was
overcome by a sort of tenderness for them. Two nurses,
Paul and Julie, Calder and Honor, and finally Dr. Martens. He increased the packing in my already crowded
nostrils. This strategy seemed to work for a minute or so,
but then the blood began to seep through my tear ducts.
My eyes glazed over with blood, and all the people in the
room faded into rosy shadows.

After a while—a long while, it seemed—one eye
cleared. In spite of my distress and the roseate hues cast
over everything by the blood in my eye, I could not help
but notice, again with something akin to tenderness,

that everyone in the room wore the same concerned look on their faces. All seven people, regardless of whether they knew me, wore the identical expression—and all seven were washed in the same rosy light. The scene was like a tableau out of antiquity. *Concern.*

Perhaps when you pray, you get people as a sort of answer. Their very presence and their need to bring comfort constitute a sort of spiritual medicine. I'm not trying to say that a miracle occurred, only that this rosy tableau of concerned faces fed into my system in some way. My body seemed to get their message: *do what you can to get better.* From that point on, something was going on inside me besides physical distress and fear and dying. It was a resolve to ride this one out. I began to resist the impulse to gulp my air and instead tried to breathe more easily. Something inside me began to turn away from imminent death.

This resolve is not courage or mental toughness or anything else mental; nor has it anything to do with miracles. It seemed to come both from my body and from the people gathered around my cot. Perhaps a sympathetic audience bestows similar gifts on a stage actor or a football team.

One of Dr. Martens's many virtues was that even at the worst of times he seemed unflappable. Everything he did appeared to be routine. Upon his arrival from South Africa he spent three years up north in Uranium City. My obdurate bodily functions were nothing new to him. He eased in the urinary catheter, and as catheters always do, this one hurt like hell. But the results were as ecstatic as a wildcat strike. I gushed urine into my catheter tube, and the relief of the people gathered around me was audible.

"Well done, Carp."

"Good show."

"Bravo."

My friends were finally persuaded to disperse and return for the night to Bob's cabin, and early in the evening they left Honor alone with me. Thus began her vigil.

For some reason I was supposed to avoid liquids during that first night in the Nipawin hospital. My throat and esophagus were raw from the irritation of so much swallowed blood. I could breathe only through my mouth. These two things made my throat and mouth chronically dry. So I was given a container of ice cubes and allowed to suck on these all through the night. Anything warmer than ice cubes could have precipitated a worse bleed.

Honor found the room chilly. She crouched by my cot with a cotton thermal blanket over her head and body. I was supposed to lie perfectly still. I clung to two fingers of her left hand. Whenever I had finished sucking another small ice cube, I would try to fall asleep. The dryness that racked my throat would awaken me. I would tug on the two fingers, and Honor would lift my nose catheter and spoon in another ice cube.

For the first ten or twenty ice cubes, I whispered, "Hank you." For the rest of the night, I merely squeezed her fingers. This woman, this wife of mine. With the white thermal blanket over her head and body, she looked vaguely Iranian.

I will never forget this picture. It's my proof for the existence of love. A small epiphany of sorts, like the moment when I flashed on the grouse bleeding from the beak, or the moment when I viewed the seven people at my bedside through blood-tinted eyeballs. I didn't see any reflections of Mary, Mother of Christ. Instead, I saw my wife looking as Muslim as the night is long.

THE NEXT MORNING I was shipped down to St. Paul's Hospital in Saskatoon. An ear, nose, and throat specialist named Dr. Will met me there. He was well named, a take-charge sort of guy. As the nurses gathered, he urged me to breathe slowly, to relax. The procedure he was about to do was going to hurt a bit, and it was going to feel very uncomfortable. I could help, he told me, by not struggling and by not doing anything that would increase my heart rate. In other words, don't panic.

Dr. Will began by yanking out a goodly length of Dr. Martens's blood-soaked packing. Instead of the saline and adrenaline solution favored by the physicians up at Nipawin, Dr. Will would use cocaine for his packing. Cocaine, I learned, promotes vasoconstriction. In went the newly powdered packing—yards of it. Then a good shot of Demerol in the rump and what must have been a huge tablet of Valium, perhaps as big as a cookie.

Well, okay, I exaggerate. Maybe the rest of this day's activities will unfold before you in hyperbolic fashion, because from this point on, I was as stoned as a New Age prophet. When Honor finally made it to Saskatoon, she came immediately to my ward. She spoke with me a while and discovered that I was scarcely able to speak, owing to my well-stuffed, well-powdered nose. Later, she said, "He looked so vulnerable. Like a deer caught in the headlights of a car."

I stayed stoned and more or less awake as the light faded in my semiprivate. I was in the safe embrace of St. Paul's Hospital. A day came when, at last, my bleeds had stopped. On Saturday, September 23, the doctor paid me one of several visits. By this time, I was off the urinary catheter, off the IV. My bodily functions were slowly kicking into gear, which meant that my body had done a turnaround: it had decided to live. The doctor checked my hemoglobin, which was better than he had expected. Then he warned me that the next little procedure would hurt a bit. With his forceps he reached in and pulled out a few inches of packing. It came and it came, like line from a reel. A yard? Two yards? At last it lay coiled and blood soaked in my kidney dish like the world's longest tapeworm, smelly with putrefaction.

I waited for the warm descent of a big clot at the back of my throat and for the blood to well up and plunge down my throat again, but there was nothing. The air rushed sweet and icy up my nostrils. A pleasure almost worth dying for. The doctor viewed my nostrils with obvious pleasure.

"How am I doing?" I said in a voice so normal it sounded abnormal.

"You're going home."

WHEN YOU COME back from a near-death experience, I am told, you might go through a sort of *oh wow* phase in which every friend, every falling leaf, every drop of rain, every dead skunk on the road is a sort of miracle of creation. My *oh wow* phase lasted a week or two. It began with my first night in bed with Honor. She had on new pajamas. The cat was purring between us. I could actually breathe through my nose.

The first day after my return, a Sunday with no wind and a brilliant blue sky, Honor made lunch for us, and we ate it on the patio. All through lunch, we watched the birds in our garden. Wrens, finches, warblers, sparrows, chickadees, a pair of woodpeckers, a raucous blue jay. They all seemed to be gathering for a smorgasbord in our garden. Pecking away at the seeds and filling up for the long winter or for the voyage south. Dozens of them, hundreds. Our perpetually enthusiastic tabby was stalking them on this day.

"He's so bad," said Honor with unguarded affection.

It's obvious our cat had made no deals with God about packing in his hunting career. For the first time in years, I was just sitting with Honor and watching birds without the slightest intention of doing anything else. Lunch would take us all afternoon. Gus the Cat moved into the rhubarb patch and crept under a huge rotting leaf.

"Look at him," I said. "Just watching."

"He's bad," said Honor.

Legions of tiny birds continued to peck and then flutter away and flutter back again at a safe distance from our murderous young cat. The sun beat down strong on our exhausted garden. The sun would soon slip into the west, we would wonder what became of it. We would comment on how this failing light sneaks up on us. We would count the *carpe diems.* They were everywhere.

NOW THAT I was at last able to shuffle around and resume my life, I had a problem to contend with. I had sworn off hunting. Honor and I were driving out to Togo to visit with Doug and Barb Elsasser. How would I tell Doug, the greatest hunter I had ever known and my hunting buddy for years, that I had taken the pledge? All morning I had been rehearsing a conversation with him.

*Ah, Doug,* I begin.

*Yeah?*

*We need to talk.*

*So? Talk.*

That's as far as I'd gotten.

The legions of geese and ducks were driving me wild. Head off in any direction from Saskatoon, wherever you could find water. There they were, flocking and fattening up, getting ready to head south. More ducks than we'd had in twenty-five years. I urged myself to learn anew how to *see* migratory fowl—in and for themselves as incomparably beautiful creatures. Not as so many succulent meals stuffed and trussed on a platter. Looks nice on paper.

These were my thoughts as Honor drove us out to Doug and Barb's place. The weather was warm, the sky cloudless. The harvest was almost entirely off the fields, and it promised to be a good one.

We turned off Highway 5 and headed south on the road to the Assiniboine Valley. This road runs through a hilly stretch filled with ranches and farms that have preserved a lot of wild brushland to the west, and a huge forest reserve in the park rises up to the east. This area had become my number one habitat for deer hunting.

Doug and Barb's place is a rambling quarter that overlooks the Lake of the Prairies. This lake is really a very long, dammed-up section of the Assiniboine River. The view from the Elsassers' cabin is expansive, to put it mildly. If you look southwest across their ravine, you can see the tip of one of their meandering fields. Some days you can spot grazing elk. If you look south and east from their kitchen, you see, instead, the Assiniboine Valley. To the north is a mixture of forest and community pasture. Straight northeast is Duck Mountain Park. This setting means whitetails, bear, wolves, and lots of other wildlife, and an abundance of game fish. Bass, muskies, pickerel, pike, perch, and five species of trout.

*Um, Doug, we need to have a talk.*

*About hunting?* he will say.

*Well, I suppose so, but it's not what you think.*

Elsasser will gawk at me.

*Something has happened,* I will say.

And then I will say...

Start over.

*Doug, we need to have a talk.*

He looks up from his cup of coffee.

*Talk? About what?*

"DOUG, WE NEED to have a talk."

We were sitting out on Doug and Barb's veranda. The autumn air was rich with stubble smells and all a-honk with passing flocks of geese. Honor and Barb were stretched out on their deck chairs, eyes closed to the warm sun. Already since breakfast we'd heard some elk bugling just below the rim of the valley. A perfect morning. For the past two or three weeks I had been looking like Death warmed over, one of Dracula's pale victims. But, like I say, it was a perfect morning.

"Is this guy-to-guy talk?" Doug said in a lazy voice.

"Fraid so."

"Well, if you two want to have a guy-to-guy talk," said Barb, "we are not movin."

She made this pronouncement through closed eyes, stroking their dog, Brewer. Brewer opened one sleepy eye, yawned, and closed his eye again.

"Let's go, Carp," said Doug. "I have to put out some leech traps. You can come along for the ride."

"And don't let him lift anything," said Honor.

Doctor's orders. Lie still and no vigorous movement. As my blood supply built up, I went everywhere slowly, like a very old man.

Doug and I climbed into Old Blue, a truck he'd had since his late teens. His leech-gathering equipment had been loaded into the back. He'd been selling these leeches to bait-and-tackle stores, which in turn would sell most of them to anglers in pickerel tournaments. It was a good sideline for Elsasser, because these days the stores paid well.

We headed on down through the gate and out across the road to a valley filled with small marshes. Perfect for leech gathering. Doug slowed down at the wheel and began to survey the nearest slough.

"Okay, Carp. What's on your mind?"

"Our annual deer hunt."

"Good. Lots of animals around this year."

"Yeah."

I took a big breath and turned to look at Elsasser. He continued to stare out at the small slough where he would lay down his first line of leech traps.

"Something happened up north," I began.

"So you've told me."

"Yeah, but I mean in addition to the bleeding and stuff."

Elsasser turned to face me. He wore a skeptical look, almost hostile, as though I were about to invite him to run for the Conservative Party of Canada.

"Have you ever been scared?" I asked him.

Elsasser was close to scoffing. "Well, I suppose I've been in situations where, you know. Where I couldn't let on what I was feeling."

"I'll take that as a yes?"

"Get to the point."

"One more question, Elsasser."

He sighed.

"When you look out at all this, the big hills, the Assiniboine Valley, all the deer, all these marshes and meadows, do you ever get to thinking what might have created it all?"

The skeptical lines of his face shifted from a "don't tell me you're workin for the Conservatives" look to a "don't tell me you've been born again" look.

"Yeah?" he said grudgingly.

"What do you call it?"

"Well, Carp, I guess I'd call it the Creator."

"Great!"

Elsasser muttered under his breath.

"When I was coming down in the car, things got sort of weird. The bleeding got kind of bad."

"So?"

"Well, I got quite worried at one point, because I was gulping blood. I mean, too much blood?"

"Yeah?"

"I couldn't stop thinking about the grouse I'd shot. The way the blood came out of his beak? So I said, like, a prayer? To the Creator?"

"Yeah?"

"And, well, I said that if he could get me out of this one alive, I'd promise never again to—"

"Oh, fuck."

"—shoot another creature."

Elsasser scowled at the gas pedal. He said, "Can I interrupt this to talk a little sense?"

"Go ahead."

"How did you word it?" said Doug, whom I'd never seen, until now, in the role of cross-examiner. "What word did you use?"

"You mean in my—"

"Yeah. Did you say fishing too?"

"Elsasser, I was worried. I wasn't crazy."

"So it's just hunting?"

"Shooting. I said I'd never shoot anything again."

"Well, does that include a bow and arrow? A rabbit stick?"

"Yeah. I think so."

"But it doesn't include fishing?"

"You don't shoot fish. And you can't do catch-and-release hunting."

Without a word, Elsasser climbed out of the truck and began to lay his leech traps. I watched him as he went. When he returned to the truck, he started it up and didn't speak for several minutes, not until we reached the top of the next grade.

"Well, Carp, I guess when you make a promise like that, you've got to keep it."

"Yeah."

"I mean, not that you had to worry all that much."

"What do you mean?"

"Well, the last few times out you couldn't hit the broad side of a barn door. I mean, hell, what is it exactly you've given up on?"

"There's no need to be sarcastic."

THAT DAY IN October was one of the loveliest times I've ever spent, not hunting, in my entire life. Perhaps I was still in my *oh wow* phase. Honor loved it in the same sweetly idle way. Doug and Barb planned a picnic supper for when the heat of the day had passed. They loaded up the car with various necessaries, including a roasted goose carefully packed away in the back trunk. Doug had shot it only a week earlier. As we drove into the heart of the Duck Mountains, the aroma of goose in the roaster moved all through the car and drove us mad with hunger.

One might think, at this point in my life, that I would have taken some sort of dietary pledge and sworn off wild meat. This did not happen. I eat much less wild meat these days, but I've never managed to sustain a vegetarian diet for more than a few weeks. The arguments against beef from feedlots are compelling, but so is the taste of curried wild goose.

We arrived at the shores of a small, deep lake surrounded by big hills and pine forest. It had heavy marshes all around the side and a small dock for canoes. We brought out the supper and the folding chairs just as the sun was beginning to set. Barb poured the wine, and with our eyes on the water, we all tucked into our Thanksgiving meal. Doug had stuffed the bird with a hot curry.

I spotted a rise near the dock, and then another.

The supper was almost too perfect to spoil with conversation, but I said, "I swear I saw a trout rise."

"Where?"

Just as I started to point, another trout rose, this time only several yards from shore, a very good fish.

"What's in the lake?" I said.

"Thought you'd never ask," said Doug, grinning. "Some rainbows and brookies."

"You're kidding."

We ate our curried goose and looked on in astonishment as the trout continued to dimple the surface. An October rise. It was almost a contradiction in terms. We felt as though it might be the last warm day of the year and the very last rise as well.

"Too bad we didn't bring our fishing gear," I said.

I detected a knowing silence, conspiratorial.

"Actually," said Honor.

"You're kidding."

Doug opened up the trunk again and took out an armload of fishing tackle. There was still time, maybe forty-five minutes before complete darkness.

"If you promise not to exert yourself," said Honor.

"I promise."

Almost three weeks had passed since I had come home from hospital, and I hadn't had enough energy, or blood, even to walk around the block. But now, with the day and the warm weather fading so beautifully, I felt a tiny surge of youth.

In another existence, perhaps I would have said no to fishing and just sat in my chair and savored the sunset and the goose curry belches and had an aesthetically satisfying moment and maybe thought briefly but deeply about mortality and life's seasonal rhythms and smoked a cigar. But of course, having learned early on that the path to hell was paved with unfished lakes, I forsook my lawn chair.

I joined Honor and Barb and Doug, fly-casting from the shore of the tiny lake. In twenty minutes we had caught and released four trout. The largest was a sixteen-inch male brookie, dazzling in dark olive and bright orange.

The day, the meal, the fishing, the people, even my confessional conversational with Elsasser at his leech traps—it had all felt like a continuous offering of thanksgiving. I had even extracted a promise from Elsasser that I would be welcome on his future hunts as a bird dog, game cleaner, cook, and plucker. I've been called worse.

## ELSASSER'S CURRIED GOOSE

1) Cook 1 cup wild rice (2½ cups water to 1 cup wild rice). Let the rice cool.

2) Heat up some cooking oil (olive, sunflower, canola— your choice) in a wok. 3 tbsp should do it.

3) Add 1 tbsp cumin, 1 tbsp soy sauce, an equal amount of shredded fresh ginger, and two chopped cloves of garlic.

4) After this mixture has been sizzling for less than 1 minute, add a large handful of chopped onion and one of chopped celery.

5) Sauté for 2 minutes or so.

6) Add two handfuls of fresh morels. If it's not spring and fresh morels aren't waiting around to be collected, add the same amount of your favorite mushrooms and continue to sauté for about 2 minutes more.

7) Add a cup or 2 of croutons or dried bread crumbs, the more savory the better.

8) Add the cooled-off wild rice.

9) Let's pretend, just this time, that our goose is a greater Canada and is still reasonably young so that it weighs no more than 7 pounds. Sprinkle the cavity with sea salt. I know, fancy schmancy; it doesn't *have* to be sea salt.

10) Spoon stuffing into the goose cavity and close up the cavity with toothpicks.

11) Start off your trussed goose, uncovered, in a large roaster, at 450°F, and after about 15 minutes, cover and reduce heat to 300°F. We are cooking this baby in a covered roaster to preserve moisture in the flesh. It's a good idea to elevate the goose on a rack so that the fat will drain to the bottom of the roaster.

12) Meditate on the brevity of life, read Thomas Mann's "Death in Venice," sample the wine you have chosen to make sure it is safe for your guests. Sample it again. Off with your clothes and call out three times, "Hail to thee, blithe spirit!" Buy two copies of this b———

My editor tells me enough already.

13) Roast covered for about 4 hours. If you want to brown it a bit more, roast uncovered for the last 15 minutes.

14) Poke roast goose with a sharp knife or equivalent. When the juice runs out clear, it is done.

# 10  THE WILD

*Teddy Roosevelt . . . poses for pictures, high-powered rifle in hand, with*
*magnificent but very dead animals deployed picturesquely around him.*
*He has shot them. A dead moose does not disturb his innocence. It is*
*unthinkable that a president would pose this way today . . . Something*
*has changed; something matured; something lived through and outlived.*

RONALD JAGER, "Hunting with Thoreau," *A Hunter's Heart*

*Such is . . . the young man's introduction to the forest, and*
*the most original part of himself. He goes thither at first as a hunter*
*and fisher, until at last, if he has the seeds of a better life in*
*him, he distinguishes his proper objects, as a poet or naturalist it*
*may be, and leaves the gun and fish-pole behind.*

HENRY DAVID THOREAU, *Walden*

WHAT HAPPENS when you fire off a Mayday to the Creator, make a deal, get through your crisis, and then renege on your part of the bargain? Do you go through the rest of your life watching your back like a Mafia informer? Do you rationalize that since you never really believed in the Creator in the first place, then a deal with Him doesn't really count? Do you cultivate superstitions about death and go around knocking on wood?

I don't know. I simply quit hunting. But can I honestly say that my departure from shooting wild game is due to a sudden religious conversion? I doubt it. My hemorrhage and its aftermath seem to have precipitated a decision not to hunt that was already forming. Perhaps it sped things up.

And yet I cannot dismiss this turning point in my life by framing it in medical terms (Narrator suffers physical trauma with weird overtones) or describing it merely as a scary mishap (Narrator has encounter with mortality but his luck holds out—whew). When I check my notes and recall the whole event, from the first bleed to the day I got out of hospital, there is a third strand to this ordeal: Narrator has serious accident and finds himself in the throes of a spiritual crisis. I had in some way found myself in Ancient Mariner territory.

Hunters are engaged in hunting down and shooting the animals they have grown to love. But to all seasoned hunters, a day must come when they find other ways to remain in touch with these creatures. Perhaps they hang around with their hunting buddies, drive them out and pick them up, help put up game, hunt down the prey with binoculars, or, as Ruthanne Hanbidge and her granddaughter have done, simply watch the animals and see how close they can come.

What happens when old hunters give their guns away, as Faulkner did, as Roderick Haig-Brown did, as Doug Elsasser's dad did, as Doug one day may do? This is a major decision in their lives, a turn in the path that has wide, archetypal implications. Whatever they do, their great love for the quarry finds a new expression, and they go from hunter to watcher to advocate. With or without epiphanies, this growth of awareness is a form of spiritual progress.

In writing this book, I keep discovering persistent patterns of spirituality among hunters past and present; I can't pretend that this stuff doesn't exist. I can no more take the spiritual communion out of hunting than I can take the pantheism out of William Wordsworth's early poetry or the transcendentalism out of Thoreau's *Walden*. Hunting can lead quite naturally to a communion with nature in the same way that hiking can, or landscape painting. Let us suppose, for a moment, that we are talking about music, not hunting. If we try to deny the spiritual element in, say, Beethoven, the blues, or Aboriginal drumming, we might also find ourselves conducting a raid on all wonder.

When I talk with Walter Linklater about his people's relationship to the earth, to the animals; when I find myself thanking the trout I have taken and cooked or taken and released; when I see the occasional hunter or angler giving thanks for a successful outing—I cannot eliminate that elusive spiritual connection. The thing that seems to bind together our most beloved and profound observers of the wilderness, regardless of religion, the thing that brings together such luminaries as Henry David Thoreau, William Faulkner, Margaret Atwood, Aldo Leopold, Annie Dillard, and José Ortega y Gasset, is their reverence for the natural world.

Reverence is respect that runs deep, and reverence

coupled with awareness goes a long way with me. If we in North America are looking for leadership in the battles to protect what remains of our most sacred hunting grounds, our most precious wildernesses, I will opt for the leader who, along with technical knowledge, scientific awareness, and political savvy and commitment, has a genuine reverence for the wilderness.

I know there will be animal rights advocates who see this argument as a desperate rationalization and who will see me as the wolf in Granny's clothing. I suspect that I have won no converts from that particular orthodoxy—because I persist in seeing some forms of hunting as part of a meaningful engagement with the wild.

When you hunt with any regularity, you also become involved in a host of other equally fascinating activities. You are learning how to observe wild animals: how they protect and care for their young, what they feed on, how they adapt to each season, how they blend in with and cohere to their habitat, how they reproduce, and how wily they must be to survive.

And you learn the woodsy craft and culinary art that follows a successful kill. You learn how to marinate wild meat, how to dress and roast a moose, how to field-dress a deer, how to hang and smoke wild meat, how to stay warm in the bush, how to track wily animals. You learn what kind of animals and birds provide the best meat. You learn which meat is better roasted, which is better smoked. You gain an intimacy with the food that will help to feed you all winter long. Never again will you take good food for granted as you have in the past. Never again will you make the mistake of assuming that food comes painlessly in packages. In every North American city I've ever visited, there are always commercial forces at work that distance you from the food you eat. Food gets spun like any other commodity and becomes anything but bloody. It becomes someone else's business. If there is any virtue in obscuring our vision of the things we eat, I have yet to discover it.

ANYWAY, THE HUNT is over for me. And I'm not alone. All over North America, hunting for sport is on the decline. Roderick Haig-Brown's predictions about the fatal impact of human proliferation on fish and game came true, but what he did not foresee is that hunting for sport, since his time, has fallen out of favor and out of fashion. According to a national survey in the United States (1995), since the time of Haig-Brown's essay in *Measure of the Year* (1950), the number of licensed hunters declined by about 75 percent. When one looks at the mighty leap in population in the United States from then until 1995, this decline in registered hunters is even more pronounced.

In a recent article, David Crary reports that this decline has continued since 1995. He is just one of a growing number of writers who predict that hunting in North America and many other regions of the world will gradually disappear. His figures (from the U.S. Wildlife Service) tell us that over the past decade, in spite of a steadily increasing population, there are 1.5 million fewer hunters in the United States. All told, that is almost sixty years of declining numbers.

One of the reasons for this decline, analysts tell us,

is the loss of hunting terrain due to urbanization. As well, more and more families are coming to the conclusion that they have little time and money for the luxury of taking their children hunting. The possibility that a father will take his kids hunting becomes even more remote in the era of the absentee father and the single-parent family. "To recruit new hunters, it takes hunting families," says Gregg Patterson of Ducks Unlimited. "I was introduced to it by my father; he was introduced to it by his father. When you have boys and girls without a hunter in the household, it's tough to give them the experience."

In some quarters, hunting has given way to shooting; safaris are organized to transport wealthy men and women to exotic locations, where they pay top dollar to kill something big. Let's remember that when Hemingway went on safaris, he walked and sweated a great deal to find his quarry. In other words, he *hunted*. The shooters I'm referring to have something easier in mind. (Yes, once again, I'm thinking of that elegant lady, *circa* 1970, in northern Scotland.)

Here's an example of what hunting has come to in my own part of the world. A former outfitter told me last year that if you want to shoot a bear in northern Saskatchewan, just find an outfitter who will bait the bears in the spring when they come out of hibernation. One outfitter he knows drives up to a branch of Robin's Donuts and asks for all the unsold goodies. He dumps these goodies into a blue barrel and drives it up north to a popular black bear habitat. In spring, when the bears come out, they are famished, and they cannot resist this free meal. As long as the outfitter renews this supply of rancid donuts, the bears will come back all through the early spring until a pattern forms and the bears become habituated. The bears learn that humans in vehicles are good for them because they feed them donuts. (Try this pedagogical approach in a national park.)

Our shooters fly in around the middle of May, when the spring hunt is in full swing. The following morning, the outfitter picks them up and drives them to a site near the killing grounds. The clients place their equipment on a quad, climb aboard, and follow the guide to a clearing in the woods where the blue barrel lies overturned and the rancid food spills out in a sumptuous mess on the ground. Two hunters are assigned to a hunting platform built among the trees, about fifteen feet above the clearing. They climb up the ladder to their roost, sit comfortably, and wait until the bears return. The guide drives his quad back to the truck and waits to hear the sound of the hunters' rifles. Or he might wait on another platform and capture the whole happy scene on camera.

He doesn't have to wait long. In a good spring, there will be a large gathering of bears under the hunters' platform, and the hunters simply select the biggest males and blast away at a distance of about forty feet. The dead bears are dragged off to the truck, and the hunters are chauffeured along with them. No one has had to do any tracking or skinning. No one has broken into a sweat. Most of the hunters are Americans, Europeans, or Canadians from large cities outside the province, and they know as little about black bear behavior and habitat when they leave as when they flew in.

Honor asked the retired outfitter if he had ever hunted in this fashion, and he told her that this new, efficient style of killing is the main reason he is no longer an outfitter.

I spoke with a group of these bear hunters a few springs ago near our cabin up north. Well-dressed men in their thirties, a pretty boisterous crew. All four men had scored a bear each, and one of them had even killed a white bear. These all-white variants are what people on the north-central coast of British Columbia refer to as spirit bears. I examined his kill and was surprised to see how small it was. My guess is about forty-four pounds, or the weight of an adult coyote.

"I know, it's only a little one," said the fellow, "but when I seen it, I said to myself, *This is the only time you'll ever see one of these bears, so make the most of it.* So I shot it."

His confession set off a chorus of laughter and ragging of the poor fellow. I felt that I had wandered into the heart of something here, so, reporter to the end, I shut my yap and did a good impersonation of a real dumb-ass. (Naïveté in the cause of information, as you've already seen, has always been one of my specialties.) And so the conversation continued.

One of the shooters was eager to impress Honor.

"I'm gonna ask our outfitter to dig out my bear's penis. You ever seen one a them?"

Honor confessed that she had not.

"Hell, they're only about yay big. I dry em out and use em for swizzle sticks. I give one to my girlfriend to stir her bar drink and she says, 'What is this thing, anyway?'

I tell her it's what I call a swizzle dick, and she says, 'A what?' And I tell her what that is, and she just about shit."

This conversation with the bear hunters takes me back to Larry Koller's advice about how to bait and kill black bears and grizzlies in the Lower Forty-eight. This practice is how the great mountain grizzlies have become endangered on both sides of the border. A century before this slaughter of mountain grizzlies, we had the mass extinction of the plains grizzlies. The tendency to kill that which we fear seems to have become a nightmare that repeats itself.

In his essay "The Violators," Jim Harrison ponders this indifference to the great denizens of the wild. "It is a very strange arrogance in man," he says, "that enables him to chase the last of the whales around the ocean for profit, shoot polar bear cubs for trophies, allow Count Blah-Blah to blast 885 pheasants in one day. It is much too designed to be called crazy or impetuous." Harrison harkens back to a time when there was a code of behavior for sportsmen and women. "Sport must be sporting. We have a strong tendency to act the weasel in the henhouse. At dawn not a single cluck was heard. It might be preposterous to think we will change, but there are signs. Judges are becoming sterner, and people are aware of environmental problems to a degree not known in [the United States] before. Game wardens get more cooperation from the ordinary citizen than they used to. Violating is losing its aura of rube cuteness."

In his study of hunters in America, David Crary concludes: "As their ranks dwindle, hunters are far from unified. The often big-spending, wide-traveling trophy hunters of Safari Club International, for example, have priorities different from duck hunters frequenting close-to-home wetlands." These words apply equally to the Canadian hunting scene. Deer and goose hunters on the Canadian prairies can bring down their legal limit with a clear conscience because deer and geese of all species are more abundant now than at any other time in recorded prairie eco-history.

Not so for other species in short supply, such as grizzlies and caribou and even grouse and duck. Big spenders can inveigle outfitters into bending the rules for the sake of killing a species at risk, and big spenders can buy their way out of trouble. I can see Faulkner and Hemingway frowning from their graves at this reality. Roderick Haig-Brown is also frowning. Jojo Mitewin is frowning. My father is frowning. Sport should be sporting.

When the number of hunters declines, other complications can arise. Valerius Geist, an environmental scientist in Calgary, has studied this phenomenon. The result of this decline is the "recolonization of wildlife." When the hunters hang up their guns, herbivores like elk, deer, and moose return in great numbers. They overgraze and exhaust their natural browse, enter the townsites in search of new places to feed, and graze in people's gardens.

The carnivores follow the herbivores—the wolves, bears, and big cats. This is phase two of animal recolonization, an example of which I've seen in my own territory. From Medicine Hat, Alberta, to Saskatoon, Saskatchewan, all along the South Saskatchewan River valley, the cougars have begun to reestablish themselves.

In both cities, we've had recent cougar sightings. In the summer of 2008, a young male cougar was shot and killed in Saskatoon in someone's backyard. Geist reports that in Yellowstone National Park in the mid-1990s, there were about fifty wolves. This population was augmented with some timber wolves imported from the Canadian North. As of this writing, the population of wolves in the Yellowstone region has swollen to more than fifteen hundred.

Phase three of animal recolonization, according to Geist, is "the parasites and diseases returning in full force." Matthew Teague, in his article on the decline of hunting in America, follows Geist's theories to the Hamptons in Long Island, home of the priciest real estate one could imagine. "The Hamptons, like a lot of New York State, are lousy with deer." Their population in Long Island is around twenty thousand—seven times what it was in the 1970s. "In Brookhaven, N.Y., officials are pondering how to handle the deer carcasses scattered across the town's roadways . . . This year they are on track to remove at least 370 deer, and the cost—at $400.00 per animal—is straining the town's budget."

After we've calculated all the damage to vehicles and human lives lost to accidents with deer, the situation gets even worse. The deer are susceptible to deer ticks, the source of Lyme disease. Suffolk County in the Hamptons "reported an estimated 585 cases last year, up from 190 two years ago."

The remedy? Licensed hunters have been hired to kill deer among the mega-homes of the Hamptons. They are urged to do this as discreetly as possible, which sometimes means night stalking and bow-and-arrow hunting. People are aware of this nocturnal predation, but few have protested. The hunters are managing to save some pretty pricey garden shrubs, they often do it for free, and the venison goes to the soup kitchens in the area.

I HAVEN'T STOPPED thinking about that paradox that dogs and defines the truest of hunters all over the world. A lobbyist against hunting might put it this way: the hunter seeks to kill that which he claims to love. A keen hunter might express it this way: hunters persist in loving that which they seek to kill.

To find some clarity in this paradox, it might help to use an analogy from our food culture. A small but growing wave of farmers, butchers, restaurateurs, chefs, and foodies have embraced the traditional pasture once again. Grass-fed beef, lamb, and pork are back, along with free-range fowl. In opposition to corporate agribusiness, which feeds corn to its cows, sends its fecal stink all over the countryside with massive feedlots, and perpetuates the fast-food burger, these old-fashioned/progressive farmers have turned their backs on all of that, turned their backs on growth hormones, artificial restraints that force cattle to be sedentary, chemicals of all kinds, in order to produce meats that actually taste like beef, pork, lamb, and chicken.

This movement is the old pastoral agrarian idyll come back to feed us once again, what Susan Bourette calls "carnivore chic." The animals on these pastures roam freely in lush grasses, graze them, and move on. The chickens follow the grazers in large numbers, digging up grubs, aerating the soil, scratching through the cattle dung for insects, thereby spreading the manure, and fertilizing the soil with their own droppings. The lush grasses soon return, and all evidence suggests that the animals and birds are happy.

Happy animals produce happy meals. Yes, the animals are slaughtered, but their voyage from pasture to butcher is considerably more humane than that of the animals that are forced to fatten up in huge feedlots, then callously slaughtered and sent to fast-food heaven. Pastured animals can be treated with love.

Hunting can be thought of in this way. People can hunt animals to extinction, claiming some kind of cultural right to do so. People can hunt with so many gadgets (helicopters, Ski-Doos, radio phones, night scopes, ATVs, SUVs, trail cameras, etc.) that they never really engage with the profound solitude of the wild. If they have enough money, people can turn hunting into mere target practice. In other words (and here comes that pagan word again), they hunt without *reverence* for the wilderness and its creatures. The animals are treated with as much love as the millions of steers that are transported from feedlots to abattoirs to produce a bacon double cheeseburger.

Or people can hunt by walking in the woods, thereby gaining a real intimacy with the wilderness. They can abide by the rules. If grizzlies or whales or sage grouse or Bengal tigers are in decline, they hunt the animals that are in good supply. Hunters can immerse themselves in the hunt and learn the habits of their quarry until that quarry is less quarry and more adversary. It's hard to respect an animal if you turn it into a target or a trophy so that you can brag about it. It's easier to love an animal if you can behold it in and of itself, and not just as a means to gratify your ego. When this transport of wonderment happens, and it happens a lot, the hunter becomes the defender of the animal and its habitat. Hunters and environmentalists who do not hunt can do some very good work together.

India has an ancient hunting tradition. It has always had its share of sporting gentlemen and poachers. Especially since the days of the British Raj, the tiger has been hunted as a status animal. Even more than the African lion, the tiger is the crown jewel of the trophy hunter's collection. At the turn of the twentieth century, an estimated forty thousand tigers lived in the wild in India. A survey in 1973 indicated that only about two thousand tigers remained. Wildlife reserves were created to protect the remaining tigers, but as the sportsmen moved out, the poachers moved in. The market for traditional medicines in China is on fire, and the trade in rare animal parts is flourishing.

Most of my information comes from Caroline Alexander's recent article in the *New Yorker*. Alexander tells us that in 2005, "every tiger in the Sariska Tiger Reserve . . . had been killed by poachers."

In India's Sundarbans Tiger Reserve, however, Alexander reports that the roughly two hundred tigers are being protected by some dedicated naturalists, hunters, and the very people in this area who are most at risk from tiger attacks: fishermen, honey collectors, wood gatherers, and other foragers from the nearby villages. Alexander interviewed a man named Mondol, whose companion had been killed by a tiger. He and two of his companions tried to scare off the tiger, but it showed no fear. "Leaping toward the victim, it caught [one of the men] by the throat and simply carried him into the forest. Mondol ran after him for some thirty or forty feet and then stopped. 'Such a big animal, but there was not a branch broken,' he said, and even before his words were translated it was possible to catch the wonderment in his voice: Not a branch, not a twig out of place." Whether former victims of tiger attacks or friends of villagers who died from tiger attacks, the people of the Sundarbans revere the tiger. As one of the wild-honey gatherers told Alexander, "If Tiger is not there, our forest will not be there, we will not get our honey."

I am not sure if the honey gatherer, above, was letting his instincts speak for him, or if he was speaking in more specifically ecological terms. But he makes sense ecologically: if we remove the top predators, their prey will become too numerous and change the habitat that produces the honey.

A naturalist named Dr. Sanyal attempted to transport a tiger out of a village that it had wandered into and return the animal to the jungle. The tiger began to wake up before they had arrived at their drop-off point, so Dr. Sanyal and his assistant had to dart it once again. Sadly, the second dosage killed the animal, and hundreds of villagers came to see it. Time and time again they said to the disconsolate Dr. Sanyal, "You could have saved this beautiful animal."

SINCE THE DAY I quit hunting I have taken many a camping trip into the wild. One warm night on the Red Deer River, Honor and I camped with our friend Grant McConnell on a small island. A full moon was rising, and the sun was going down, and we three sat around a campfire. Our tents were set up, and we were about to turn in when Grant pointed toward the sunset and repeated those immortal lines from the movies: "Uh-oh, I think we got company."

We looked to where Grant was pointing as two big moose trotted ashore, a cow and a bull, their magnificent bodies eclipsing the sunset. Suddenly our little island seemed a lot smaller.

The moose moved cautiously past us and went into the willows about a hundred yards behind us. They were bedding down for the night a stone's throw from our tents! I began to wonder just how territorial a moose might get in the middle of the night.

We had a brief discussion and decided to load up quickly and find ourselves another island. We didn't take long to abandon the site. Thank God we had a full moon.

But what might have happened if one of us had brought a rifle along for security? Would this have led to a couple of moose carcasses rotting on an island in the summer heat? A threatened or injured bull moose rampaging through our campsite?

In January of 2007, Honor and I were snowshoeing along the upper rim of the Beaver Creek coulee, heading for the place where Beaver Creek runs into the South Saskatchewan River. Across the creek to the south, perhaps three hundred yards away, some big farm dogs were barking. We paid them no attention, but they kept up with their barking and would not leave the farmyard. Something was not right. Why would farm dogs bark at us from such a distance, and why would these big dogs not dare to leave their yard by the farmhouse?

Honor and I continued tromping through the snow until at last we reached the outlook. We could now gaze back up the coulee that housed the creek or out onto the river and beyond at the vast expanse of scrub and parkland hills that rose up from the valley. Honor was checking out the upper valley, and I was looking down at the confluence of frozen creek and river. The barking of the dogs was now less insistent. I recall that Honor and I were talking about something.

Just then, from a thick tangle of cattails and willows perhaps sixty feet below me, a great gray dog leapt out and took off with furious speed. Not a dog, a huge overgrown gray coyote. No, not a coyote, a wolf. It was a timber wolf big enough to gulp down a coyote of any size, big enough to snack on beavers or dogs. It tore away from us and raced around the far bank of the creek and disappeared into the next coulee.

While Honor gazed into the opposite distance, I choked out something like: "Oh, son of a bitch, I don't friggin believe it. Holy great groaning grunions, did you see the . . ."

Honor was now looking to where I pointed.

"The what?" she said.

Never have I wanted more for a hiking companion to see what I saw, but all she saw were the wolf's tracks on the ice of Beaver Creek.

What if I'd had my old 30/30 at the ready? What would we have here? A dead wolf at the bottom of a coulee? A wounded wolf limping off into the bush to die? And if I'd killed it, what would I have done with this magnificent dead predator? Would I have stuffed it? Why in God's name would I have stuffed a wolf carcass? To show how brave and woodsy I was? To show my friends that Carp still had the old hunter's instinct? Perhaps all I'm saying is that, as happens to old hunters, the rifle has slipped from my grasp.

What I did do was go home and study up on wolf behavior in my neck of the woods. I had never even heard of wolves on the prairie, where they used to roam a century before. I soon found out that wolves were just beginning to show up again in isolated pockets all across the Canadian prairie. Ephemeral family groups, they are called. I already knew that, for about a decade now, moose had been relocating from the northern forest to the grainfields of the prairie in impressive numbers. Were the wolves at last beginning to follow that migration? Were they simply going after the mule deer and whitetails that have multiplied with such great success on the prairies? Probably.

I also discovered that young male wolves are sometimes forced to leave their family units and fend for themselves. The alpha males send the younger males off sometimes because the deer population is down where the family has been foraging. When the deer return in good numbers, the lone wolves are welcomed back into the fold.

But my Beaver Creek wolf was an isolated incident, and I had almost forgotten this rare sighting when, in February of 2007, Honor and I went on a writer-and-artist's retreat to St. Peter's Abbey, a monastery near Muenster, Saskatchewan. It's my favorite place for finishing manuscripts. Honor works there on drawings, photography projects, and paintings. The abbey is a bit more than an hour's drive across the prairie, east of Saskatoon. It is set in farmland, but there are great stretches of bush and heavy trees that line both sides of the Wolverine Creek valley and planted trees that serve as windbreaks for the crops in the fields.

In the winter of 2006–07 we'd had a huge dump of snow. It came so early and piled up so deep that certain crops, planted late because of excessive spring rains, were not harvested. One such crop was some organic Marquis wheat on the abbey property. Our bedroom in the abbey guest wing looked out in an easterly direction at this unharvested field and the trees surrounding it. As we were preparing for bed, Honor and I heard some howling right outside our window. Not only was the howling very close by; it was in a sonorous register much too low for coyotes.

Oh, no, I'm not biting. This is not a wolf. No, no—this would be absolutely too much, and besides, after I had spotted a wolf at Beaver Creek, scarcely ten miles south of Saskatoon, no one would believe me.

"What is that low howling?" said Honor. "Is that a coyote?"

"Yes," I said, "it has to be a coyote."

"Seems awful close," she said.

I am not biting. This is definitely not a wolf. This is just a lone coyote with a low voice. Too old to hit the high notes. That is what it is.

Honor and I made a point of visiting with Father Demetrius the next morning. We mentioned the howling.

"Oh, yes," he said, "that's our wolf."

"Don't you mean coyote?" said Honor.

"No," said Demetrius, "I mean wolf."

He told us a story about a drive he and Father Paul had taken about a month earlier. The snow was unusually deep from a series of recent blizzards. There had been reports of a wolf hanging around in the Wolverine Creek area. At least half a dozen people around there had spotted it. And as they were approaching the abbey, driving east on Highway 5, Father Paul cried out, "There it is!"

Several whitetails were leaping across a field and heading for the highway. Behind them was a huge, dark timber wolf. It was attempting to cut the deer off before they reached the highway, but it kept breaking through the snow's light crust and slowing down. The deer were able to navigate in the deep snow, perhaps because they had longer legs. Perhaps as well, they were able to stay on top of the crust because of how their body weight was distributed.

Father Demetrius brought the car to a stop. The wolf watched as the deer pranced, unscathed, across the highway.

I sought out others who had seen the animal, and they all agreed that it was way too big and darkly colored to be a coyote. It was a timber wolf. Some, including Father Demetrius, claimed it was black.

He walked with us out into the deep snow. He wanted us to know that this creature was no coyote, and he claimed to have evidence. We followed his black cassock as it whipped about in the wind. He led us into a long windbreak made up of blue spruce and some big golden willows with yellow branches. Beside one of these large trees, Demetrius came to a halt.

"Most of them are covered up with snow, but this one is more recent."

He was standing over a large deer carcass. Its insides had been torn out and eaten—all but the stomach, which lay like a small stuffed bag by the gaping ribcage. All around the kill site were animal prints. They looked as if they belonged to a pack of neighborhood dogs. But one set of prints was much larger than any of the others. Think Great Dane or Newfoundland.

"You said most of them are covered up with snow," I inquired. "You mean prints?"

"No," said Demetrius, who turned to go back to the residence. "I mean kill sites."

"Plural?"

"I think there are at least a dozen."

The word spread, and we gathered together a nice troop of artists and writers for an excursion after work. We donned our snowshoes, skis, and snow boots and trekked from one kill site to another. I think we found seven or eight, some of which were still uncovered, because the coyotes kept coming back to gnaw at the bones of the fallen deer.

During such a harsh winter, the unharvested crop of Marquis wheat was a godsend to all the whitetails that gathered each night to feed. The herd numbered up to a hundred or so animals. But the deer that gathered on the field were in turn a veritable banquet to the wolf and the coyotes whose cries we heard each night. The wolf was always first to howl, and the coyotes would answer with falsetto choruses of their own. It wasn't hard to hear the difference between the cries of the two species. Wolves howl and coyotes yip. The wolf can get up near the coyotes' falsetto now and then, but it's more comfortable in a lower range. The coyotes own the upper register, and their yipping can cover an astonishing range of notes and vocabulary. But when they go off together, one wolf and a pack of coyotes sound like a canine chamber group for a dozen clarinets and one bassoon.

How did these two species relate out here on the prairie? They were clearly both feeding on the deer, but coyotes do not join up with wolves under any circumstances. One hears rumors of wolves and coyotes mating up north, but there is very little evidence for this behavior, and all of it comes from Eastern Canada. Wolves (from the northern boreal forest) and coyotes (from the southern prairie) are rivals for the same food and territory. A coyote that teams up with a wolf for mating or any other purpose would have to have a death wish.

Honor took an early morning ski from the abbey to the Muenster townsite via the railway tracks. She came back with an interesting discovery. She had found some fresh tracks made by deer during the night. The deer tracks were followed by the tracks of seven coyotes. The coyote tracks were occasionally visited by a sprinkling of monster tracks made by something much larger. Again, think Newfoundland or Great Dane.

I could not escape the notion that, between these predators, there might be some sort of symbiosis, that even if they were sworn enemies, they were hunting together in some way. Or at the very least, their howls and yipping kept them in contact with each other so that, once the wolf had had its fill, the coyotes could move in and feast on the remains of the deer.

One or two nights later, Demetrius took his usual midnight walk from the church to the spot where the railway tracks and the highway come together. This walk took him right to the north of the field where sixty to seventy deer were feeding. They were easy for him to spot, dark silhouettes against the white of the deep snow. He made it past the field to the northeastern edge of the windbreak, and there, among the blue spruce, was an entire pack of coyotes. And not fifty feet away was the black wolf.

One thing you learn about Demetrius is that he is very tough. He is no stranger to hardship, pain, death, and physical danger. He does not need a rifle to bolster his courage. And so he stood there, all alone but for the deer herd behind him and the coyotes in front of him, and he stared right into the eyes of his wolf.

Everything out there that night on the abbey grounds, it seemed, was eating or getting eaten. Father Demetrius turned his back on the wolf and its smaller cousins and walked back to the abbey.

I never saw the wolf, but believe me, tracking him and putting together the forensics of how the coyotes

followed the wolf to cash in on the meal were as fascinating as any hunt I've ever been on. Hunting taught me
to pay attention, and the rewards of paying attention to
the natural world are just as profound as ever.

I MENTION THIS in a month when, for the first time
ever, there are no guns in our house. My trusty sixteen-
gauge, the one my dad gave me when I turned seventeen,
is now in the hands of Doug Elsasser.

I still get a kick out of shooting arrows at targets. For
this I need a longbow, a traditional bow. I've been working away at how to tiller these traditional bows. Tillering
is simply the act of shaving wood from a stave where the
stave doesn't bend enough or leaving wood on the stave
where it might bend too much. Tillering is the bowyer's
way of carving with care.

From time to time I go out and gather some wild
green ash or chokecherry, trees that in most cases are
doomed to be bulldozed away by someone else. These
two kinds of wood make excellent bows because they are
flexible, strong, and light—ideal for carving. If the wood
is treated properly, a bow made from chokecherry can
last a long time. I fashion my bows from three to five feet
long, because this is about the size of the ones the great
bison hunters of the distant past used on the prairies.

The Native hunters used deer sinew for strings; I use
cord that I salvage from various household items—old
venetian blinds, for example.

Two of my creations, so far, have been mildly successful, but I have no intention of using them to hunt
anything. For me, making bows and shooting them is a

substitute for hunting. But perhaps it is more than a substitute, because making a bow grounds me in the sort of history from which you, dear reader, and I have evolved.

One day when I was hauling away a recently bull-dozed green ash, I stopped to examine it. I brought out a knife and proceeded to hack away the branches and then to peel away the bark. I examined the stave I was left with for its potential as a longbow. I was in a leafy clearing on a hot day, and for some reason I looked up. A deer was watching me, a mature whitetail doe with no fawns around. In spite of the weapon I was fashioning, I was apparently no threat to her. *You going to shoot that thing, little fella?* she might have said. *Lotsa luck, eh.* Her tail did not go up. She just walked off a ways and returned to grazing. I can't help wondering how she would have regarded me during the days when I was a keen hunter of her species.

If I were a hunter now, I would hunt with a longbow. I admire the persistence and skill of the traditional bowyer/hunters that take to the woods all over this continent, especially in the Deep South.

It makes little sense to me to shoot doves as they do down there. Are these birds just targets, or is there some deeper cultural engagement going on? It makes little sense to me to shoot a bear from the safety of a platform so that you can take its pelt and turn its penis into a swizzle stick. It makes no sense to me to pursue Bengal tigers or snow leopards or grizzlies just to kill them. But where I live, it makes eminent good sense to hunt for whitetails, mule deer, feral hogs, snow geese, and Canada honkers. They were once in short supply, or ample supply, and now they may well be in oversupply. And in all cases, with the usual careful preparation, their meat is wonderful.

I know a young man from my neighborhood named Liam. He is fourteen years old. His grandfather has encouraged him to take a hunter safety course and to get his beginner's hunting license. He is very well coordinated, he learns fast, and he's hell on clay pigeons. He is probably the only young person I know around here who wants to hunt. I want him to become one of those hunters who become guardians of habitat, who walk the woods with reverence, and who gain a great abiding love for the wild creatures they pursue. I know his grandfather, and so my hopes for Liam seem entirely reasonable.

Little man, good hunting to you.

# SOURCES

THIS BOOK reflects more time in the woods and fields than in the stacks. Nevertheless, to write it, I have had to read my way into some pretty exciting territory. I have listed my sources below, chapter by chapter, in order of their appearance, or the shadow of their influence, in my text. This shadow includes books I haven't quoted from but which might have broadened my approach to this subject.

CHAPTER 1 *That Good Old Time*
Page 31 Jared Diamond, *Guns, Germs, and Steel*, New York: W.W. Norton & Company, 1997, p. 43. Diamond reminds us that the dodo bird has become "virtually a symbol of extinction" by human hands. His book is a fascinating look at the calamities and accidents of world history, but this is history as seen by an anthropologist who knows a lot about environmental science. Diamond throws in a little chaos theory for good measure. For the purposes of this book, I found parts 1 and 2 particularly interesting.

Page 32 See Throckmorton's comments in Matthew Teague, "A More Dangerous Game," *Sports Illustrated*, November 24, 2008, p. 64.

CHAPTER 2 *Skulking through the Bushes*
Page 34 Michael Pollan, *The Omnivore's Dilemma*, New York: Penguin Books, 2006, p. 314. This book is a delightful compendium of what we eat and a well-aimed critique targeted not only at corporate food production but also at our own eating habits. I suspect that the spirit of Pollan's book haunts

several of my chapters. His follow-up book, *In Defense of Food,* is a decidedly contemporary yet delightfully old-fashioned vision of what constitutes good food.

Pages 36–42  My account of the earliest evolution of hunting was guided by a number of sources. The conclusions to many of these inquiries are fraught with speculation and politics, as Elaine Dewar reminds us in her thoughtful book *Bones,* Toronto: Vintage Canada, 2001. Therefore, the historian needs to ride through this territory with some care. One of the better sources for dietary and paleoanthropological details is the website www.beyondveg. com. I was able to glean some helpful facts about human and hunter evolution from two learned and readable books by Stephen J. Gould: *Dinosaur in a Haystack,* New York: Harmony Books, 1995, Chapters 19 and 27; and *Wonderful Life,* New York: W.W. Norton & Company, 1989, Chapter 1. Also helpful on questions of evolution was Donald Johanson and Blake Edgar's *From Lucy to Language,* New York: Simon & Schuster, 1996, Chapter 15.

Page 36  For a summary of the hunting hypothesis, see Matt Cartmill, *A View to a Death in the Morning,* Cambridge, MA: University of Harvard Press, 1993, p. 14.

Pages 39–42  There is a wide assortment of facts available to readers on the encroachment of agrarian practices upon the hunter-gatherer cultures throughout the world in Richard B. Lee and Richard Daly (eds.), *The Cambridge Encyclopedia of Hunters and Gatherers,* Cambridge: Cambridge University Press, 1999. See especially pp. 90, 388, and 389.

Page 40  Trevor Herriot, *Jacob's Wound,* Toronto: McClelland & Stewart, 2004, pp. 62–63. This book is Herriot's search for the spirit of wildness, a tough but inspiring read and an unapologetically moral approach to history and wilderness. Herriot's book is my best source of information on the Hakkarmel burial sites in Israel, and it helped give me some perspective on my approach to the evolution of hunting.

Page 42  Jared Diamond, *Guns, Germs, and Steel,* p. 46.

Page 43  Liz Bryan, *The Buffalo People,* Edmonton: University of Alberta Press, 1991, pp. 32–33. A very engaging study and a joy to read. Bryan's work helped me round out my history of subsistence hunting and bring it home to the Canadian prairies. Some of the hunting facts on pp. 44–45 are taken from her book and from my correspondence with Trevor Herriot. My research on Native bows and arrows came from my discussions with Plains Cree historians and elders.

Pages 44–49  Theodore Binnema, *Common and Contested Ground*, Toronto:
University of Toronto Press, 2004. This history of the northwestern plains
helped me with a number of details, especially in getting the timelines right
for the evolution of horsemanship, hunting, and warring on the Great Plains.
Also helpful was J. Edward Chamberlin, *Horse: How the Horse Has Shaped
Civilizations*, Toronto: Alfred A. Knopf Canada, 2006, Chapters 1–3.

Pages 48–49 and 51–52  Roger Longrigg, *The History of Foxhunting*, New
York: Clarkson N. Potter, 1975. In his opening chapter, Longrigg takes a
look at the point in human history where sport hunting branched off from
the rigors of subsistence hunting. In the remaining chapters, this book is not
so much about hunting as about manners, apparel, style, and lineage
(horses, dogs, and fox hunters).

Page 50  David Petersen (ed.), *A Hunter's Heart*, New York: Owl Books, 1997.
Petersen's book is an anthology of thoughtful, conscience-ridden accounts
of hunting, primarily in the United States. Less bang em 'n bag em and more
vigilance in the cause of wildlife, and an ethical approach ("fair chase") to
hunting. I recommend this book to all kinds of readers, including hunters
whose fascination with the sport goes beyond techniques, brand names, and
gadgetry, to the wildlife itself.

Page 50  Rick Bass, *Caribou Rising*, San Francisco: Sierra Club Books, 2004.
Bass is a joy to read, whether he is speaking of his own region, the Yaak
Valley of Montana, or traveling some other wilderness. He is a fervent
protector of habitat and hunting cultures.

Page 50  James Swan, *In Defense of Hunting:* San Francisco, Harper, 1995.
Swan's book is an important contribution to hunting literature. At times he
becomes almost unduly defensive about sport hunting among modern
middle-class nimrods; a writer can only push suburban primitivism so far.
For the most part, however, hunting and Jungian analysis seem to go
nicely together in this book.

Pages 52–53  See Paul Theroux, "Thoreau on the Moose," *Los Angeles Times*,
September 14, 2008.

Page 53  Ralph H. Lutts, *The Nature Fakers* (revised edition), Charlottesville,
VA: University Press of Virginia, 2007, p. 12.

Pages 54–56  Aldo Leopold, *A Sand County Almanac*, New York: Oxford University Press, 1948. This book, with admirable line drawings by Charles W.
Schwartz, is a latter-day Thoreauvian wonder, a true classic. I drew some

good hunting and conservation wisdom from part III, "The Upshot." See especially pp. 177–178.

CHAPTER 3 *The Forest Primeval*
Page 59 "This is the forest primeval." These lines are from the opening stanza of Henry Wadsworth Longfellow's *Evangeline*.

Page 59 Roderick Haig-Brown, *Measure of the Year*, Don Mills, ON: William Collins Sons, 1950, p. 191.

Page 71 Matthew Teague, "A More Dangerous Game," *Sports Illustrated*, November 24, 2008, pp. 64–65.

CHAPTER 4 *The Dawning of Ambivalence*
Page 74 T.J. Schwanky, "Trail Cameras," *The Outdoor Edge*, Jan.–Feb. 2007, Vol. 17, Issue 1, pp. 6–7.

Page 74 C.L. Rawlins, "I Like to Talk about Animals," in David Petersen's *A Hunter's Heart*, New York: Owl Books, 1997, p. 93.

Pages 76–80 Larry Koller, *The Treasury of Hunting*, New York: Odyssey Press, 1965.

Pages 81–84 Ernest Hemingway, *Green Hills of Africa*, New York: Charles Scribner's Sons, 1935. This work of literary nonfiction is based on journals Hemingway kept during his first safari to Africa. It reminds me that although Hemingway was training himself to become a novelist, he was a very good journalist.

References to this work and Hemingway's *Death in the Afternoon* (1932) are taken from Sean Hemingway (ed.), *Hemingway on Hunting*, Guilford, CT: The Lyons Press, 2001. References to Hemingway's short stories are from *The Complete Short Stories of Ernest Hemingway*, The Finca Vigia Edition, New York: Charles Scribner's Sons, 1987. These stories might serve to remind readers of that little-publicized side to Hemingway that is downright tender and humane. Try "A Clean, Well-Lighted Place" and "Hills Like White Elephants."

Pages 84–90 William Faulkner, *Go Down, Moses*, New York: First Vintage International Edition, 1990, pp. 181–315. This classic of American fiction is a linked sequence of stories that reads like a novel, because each story enriches each other story. In addition to the famous novella "The Bear,"

there are two other fine hunting stories in this volume: "The Old People"
and "Delta Autumn." Details from Faulkner's life come from several sources,
but the best for this project was Jay Parini's biography of Faulkner, *One
Matchless Time*, New York: HarperCollins, 2004. Readers interested in pursuing the life of Boon Hogganbeck might want to read Faulkner's novel *The
Reivers*. Steve McQueen stars in the movie version. As Boon Hogganbeck,
he stinks.

Page 85  Jay Parini, *One Matchless Time*, p. 305.

Pages 90–93  Roderick Haig-Brown, *Measure of the Year*, Don Mills, ON:
William Collins Sons, 1950, pp. 185–191. This fascinating book should be
read by lovers of Aldo Leopold's *A Sand County Almanac* and vice versa. Most
details on Haig-Brown's life are from Valerie Haig-Brown, *Deep Currents*,
Victoria, BC: Orca Book Publishers, 1997. Among the many delights of this
book, by one of Haig-Brown's daughters, is an account of his courtship of
Ann Elmore, including generous quotations from their love letters.

Page 91  Roderick Haig-Brown, *Panther*, London: Collins, 1967. This book
first came out in 1934, and that same year an American edition was released
under the title of *Ki-yu*. Once promoted as juvenile fiction, the novel is
almost too gritty for youthful readers. I could not put it down.

CHAPTER 5 *Throwbacks*
Page 98  Alberto Manguel, *The City of Words*, Toronto: Anansi, 2007, p. 56.

Page 116  Matthew Teague, "A More Dangerous Game," *Sports Illustrated*,
November 24, 2008, p. 60.

CHAPTER 6 *The Return of Artemis*
Page 117  Mary Zeiss Stange, *Woman the Hunter*, Boston: Beacon Press, 1997,
pp. 184–185.

Pages 121–123  On the subject of Aboriginal women hunting either with
or without men, see Richard B. Lee and Richard Daly (eds.), *The Cambridge
Encyclopedia of Hunters and Gatherers*, pp. 411–416.

Page 123  Readers might wonder whether there are any accounts of Aboriginal women, *by* Aboriginal women, that describe the hunt. I could find very
little evidence of these accounts from the nineteenth century, but Louise
Erdrich, who has Aboriginal roots, writes a riveting story of Native hunting
in *Tracks*, New York: HarperCollins, 1988.

Page 124  Deborah Homsher, *Women & Guns: Politics and the Culture of Firearms in America*, New York: M.E. Sharpe, 2001, p. 64. In Homsher's discussion of firearms among Aboriginal males on the Great Plains in the nineteenth century, she refers to the work of Alan Klein. See p. 77 for complete details.

Page 124  The increase in numbers of North American women who now hunt is discussed in Mary Zeiss Stange and Carol K. Oyster, *Gun Women*, New York: New York University Press, 2000, pp. 23–24. See also Stange's essay, "Look Who's Stalking" in *Outdoor Life*, May 1998, pp. 62 and following. Homsher questions these figures in *Women & Guns*. See the chapter entitled "Fields Near Home."

Page 124  Mary Zeiss Stange, "Look Who's Stalking," *Outdoor Life*, pp. 62 and following.

Page 125  Theodore Roosevelt, "The Strenuous Life," in *The Works of Theodore Roosevelt*, Vol. xii, New York: Charles Scribner's Sons, 1926, p. 4.

Pages 125–126  Stange, *Woman the Hunter*, p. 76.

Page 126  Stange, *Woman the Hunter*, p. 71.

Page 128  Homsher, *Women & Guns*, pp. 16–17.

Pages 128–129  Homsher, *Women & Guns*, p. 71.

Page 130  See Jake MacDonald's article "The Autumn's Glass," in *Conservator*, 2007 Waterfowling Heritage Issue, pp. 20–23.

Pages 130–135  I taped my interview with Ruthanne and Barbara Hanbidge on February 6, 2009.

Page 133  On the historical roots of trophy hunting, see Greg Gillespie's essay in Jean L. Manore and David G. Miner (eds.), *The Culture of Hunting in Canada*, Vancouver: UBC Press, 2007, pp. 42–55. The essays in this volume are written primarily by academics, but the jargon is kept to a minimum in most of these papers. I found a number of them very helpful. In "Hunting Stories," Peter Kulchyski writes about the cultural importance for Aboriginal people of the annual hunt. He contrasts Aboriginal and white attitudes to hunting and has some interesting observations to make on the subject of Aboriginal women hunting. Using different sources for his research, Bruce Hodgins makes a similar argument in "Aboriginal Peoples and Their Historic Right to Hunt." In his essay, "The Empire's Eden," Greg Gillespie has much to say about the impact on sport hunting in North America of the English gentleman, whose code of sportsmanlike hunting had much to do with social class, which meant exclusive hunting rights. The New World became for him a culturally constricted colonial space. He justified his collection of trophy heads in terms of their value to science. Roland Bohr's interview with Louis Bird, "Views of a Swampy-Cree Elder," is a very good way of easing into Native spirituality and the conservation ethic that arises from these beliefs. With regional variations, they apply to many Aboriginal peoples in North America and not just the northern Cree hunters. David Calverly's essay, "When the Need for It No Longer Existed," is critical of past government conservation programs in Ontario. I found it disconcerting to learn the extent to which the economy had dictated how wildlife was protected. Jean Manore's essay on Algonquin Park, "Contested Terrains of Space and Place," is about different attitudes to nature. One such view, which comes to us from nineteenth-century American writers, argues that the wilderness experience tends to encourage self-reliance, manliness, and individuality. Edward Reid ("Personal Expression as Exemplified by Hunting") argues with some conviction that sport hunters can feel some of the passionate spirituality most often ascribed to Aboriginal hunters. He would like to bring back the spring bear hunt to Ontario. I have to assume that he is dead set against bear baiting. Tim Sopuck brings animal activists into the picture with "The Activists Move West." He recounts the opposition from activists to penned hunting and to the annual spring bear hunts in Ontario and Manitoba. Edward Hanna, in "Fair Chase," traces the ethical evolution of fairness in, primarily, sport hunting and offers a wide-ranging account of hunting culture and a sanely ecocentric approach to the pursuit and protection of wildlife.

CHAPTER 7 *The Last Great Hunter*
Page 136  James Welch, *Fools Crow*, New York: Penguin Books, 1987, pp. 123, 164, and 356. James Welch came from the Blackfoot First Nation in Montana. He wrote five novels before his death in 2003. Welch's research into the lives of the nineteenth-century Plains Indians, for the writing of this novel, is as meticulous as that of any historian I have ever read. *Fools Crow* is the winner of three major literary awards, including the Los Angeles Times Book Prize.

Page 148  Hugh Brody, *The Other Side of Eden: Hunters, Farmers and the Shaping of the World*, Vancouver: Douglas & McIntyre, p. 5.

240 · A HUNTER'S CONFESSION

Pages 149–150 Jerry Haigh, *The Trouble with Lions*, Edmonton: The University of Alberta Press, 2008. Haigh is not only a dedicated conservationist, he is a riveting storyteller.

Pages 150–151 Quotations from Louis Bird, as recorded by Roland Bohr, are from Jean L. Manore and Dale G. Miner's (eds.), *The Culture of Hunting in Canada*, Vancouver: UBC Press, 2007, p. 102.

Pages 151–153 I talked with Walter Linklater at his home in Saskatoon primarily from June to August of 2008.

Pages 151–152 Adrian Tanner, *Bringing Home Animals*, Corner Brook, NL: Institute of Social and Economic Research, 1979, Chapters 6, 7, and 8. What Tanner says about religious beliefs among the Mistassini Cree hunters tallies nicely with what Hugh Brody, Louis Bird, and Walter Linklater have said about how northern Aboriginal people respected the animals they hunted.

Pages 153–154 Hugh Brody, *The Other Side of Eden*, p. 5. Readers who want to pursue the subject of Aboriginal hunter-gatherer communities will find Hugh Brody's books accessible and very enlightening. Brody has spent many years of his life hunting with seal, caribou, and moose hunters all over the Canadian North—indeed, with hunting people all over the world. He dedicates himself to learning as much of the Aboriginal languages as he can. Inspiring work.

Page 155 I am quoting Trevor Herriot from a note he sent me in the spring of 2008.

Pages 155–159 Mathieu Mestokosho in Serge Bouchard, *The Caribou Hunter*, trans. Joan Irving, Vancouver: Greystone Books, 2006, pp. 65–66. This page-turner gives a close-up narration of Aboriginal hunting in Labrador, mostly for caribou in winter. To see how vigorous and dedicated this life was, before the advent of snowmobiles, gives the uninitiated reader a heart-stopping respect for these Innu hunters.

Page 159 I am referring primarily to J. Edward Chamberlin, *If This Is Your Land, Where Are Your Stories?*, Toronto: Vintage, 2004, and *The Harrowing of Eden: White Attitudes toward North American Natives*, Toronto: Fitzhenry and Whiteside, 1975, as well as Barry Lopez, *About This Life*, Toronto: Random House of Canada, 1998.

Page 159 To read a historical view of the conflicted schemes of Canadian conservationists to preserve wildlife in the Northwest Territories, a movement that often had a bad impact on Aboriginal hunters, see John Sandlos, *Hunters at the Margin: Native People and Wildlife Conservation in the Northwest Territories,* Vancouver: UBC Press, 2007.

Pages 159–160 Elie Dolgin, "Hello, Dolly," *The Globe & Mail,* May 3, 2008.

Page 160 Ian McAllister, *The Last Wild Wolves.* Vancouver: Greystone Books, 2007. McAllister offers a courageous account of people studying wolves as unobtrusively as possible. The book comes with stunning photographs and a CD of wolves filmed days before they were shot and killed by an outfitter. In the process of breaking your heart, this book will inspire you.

Pages 160–161 Barry Lopez, *Arctic Dreams,* New York: Charles Scribner's Sons, 1986, pp. 273–274.

Page 161 Of all the classic texts I've ever read on wilderness, Henry David Thoreau's *Walden* is the Bible. To sample what Thoreau can do, just try his chapter entitled "Spring." If you feel like a little weekend transcendence, this guy will take you there.

CHAPTER 8 *Pleasure*
Page 165 José Ortega y Gasset, *Meditations on Hunting,* trans. Howard B. Wescott, New York: Charles Scribner's Sons, 1972, p. 138. Do not read this wise and eccentric book to learn how the hunter comes to love and defend the prey and its habitat. This philosophical treatise focuses exclusively on the hunter as predator.

Pages 167–168 Richard Ford, "Hunting with My Wife," *Sports Afield,* Winter 1996–97. For readers of contemporary fiction who also like hunting stories, Ford's early novel *A Piece of My Heart,* London: Collins Harvill, 1987, is a delight.

Page 168 Note from Trevor Herriot, spring of 2008.

Page 170 Hugh Brody, *Maps and Dreams,* Vancouver: Douglas & McIntyre, 1981. This book is an inspired voyage into the visionary world and the wisdom of Aboriginal hunter-gatherers. Robert Brightman, *Grateful Prey,* Regina: Canadian Plains Research Centre, 2002. This reads like a book by an academic written for other academics. Too bad the jargon is so dense, because Brightman really has something to say.

Page 171  Susan Bourette, *Carnivore Chic*, Toronto: Viking Canada, 2008, pp. 104–105. Bourette takes us on a quest in search of the most sumptuous meat she can find. Her book (although less scholarly) is written in the spirit of Michael Pollan's *The Omnivore's Dilemma*. Very informative, and it gives one's salivary glands a nice workout. If you've ever considered becoming a lapsed vegetarian, this is the book for you.

Pages 181–182  José Ortega y Gasset, *Meditations on Hunting*, p. 132.

CHAPTER 9 *Blood*
Page 184  Samuel Taylor Coleridge, *Lyrical Ballads*, Second Edition, London: Pearson Longman, 2007, p. 391.

Pages 184–204  The events from Chapter 9 are recounted in altered form and greater detail in an earlier book of mine, *Courting Saskatchewan*, Vancouver: Greystone, 1996.

CHAPTER 10 *The Wild*
Page 207  Ronald Jager, "Hunting with Thoreau," in David Petersen's *A Hunter's Heart*, New York: Owl Books, 1997, p. 77.

Page 207  Brooks Atkinson (ed.), *Walden and Other Writings of Henry David Thoreau*, New York: Modern Library, 1992, p. 200.

Pages 211–212, 215–216  David Crary, "Across U.S., Hunt's On for Aspiring Hunters," *San Antonio Express-News*, September 7, 2007.

Page 211  For more details of the survey on licensed hunters, see James Swan, *In Defense of Hunting*, San Francisco: Harper, 1995, p. 3.

Pages 215, 216  Jim Harrison, "The Violators," in David Petersen's *A Hunter's Heart*, p. 218.

Page 216  In a note, spring 2008, Trevor Herriot reminded me that whitetail deer did not exist on the open plains until we managed to wipe out the buffalo and suppress prairie fires.

Page 216–218  Matthew Teague, "A More Dangerous Game," *Sports Illustrated*, November 24, 2008, pp. 61–62. See also Jan E. Dizard, *Mortal Stakes*, Boston: University of Massachusetts Press, 2003, pp. 26–27. Teague's account of the proliferation of whitetails in and around the Hamptons and the health dangers they have brought with them picks up where Dizard's account leaves off.

Pages 220–221  Caroline Alexander, "Tigerland," *The New Yorker,*
April 21, 2008, pp. 66 and following.

Pages 230–231  Hunters interested in going the traditional bow route,
and in learning how to tiller a bow for themselves, should read Jim
Hamm (ed.), *The Traditional Bowyer's Bible,* Volumes 1–3, New York:
Bois d'Arc Press, 1992.

**DAVID CARPENTER** is the author of eight books of fiction, including *Niceman Cometh* and *Welcome to Canada*, and two nonfiction books, *Fishing in Western Canada* and *Courting Saskatchewan*. His fiction and his essays have won seven literary awards. He lives and writes in Saskatoon, Saskatchewan.